Read the World through News in English

Takayuki Ishii Takashi Kita

[proofreader] Ted Ostis

SANSHUSHA

音声ダウンロード＆ストリーミングサービス（無料）のご案内

https://www.sanshusha.co.jp/text/onsei/isbn/9784384335262/

本書の音声データは、上記アドレスよりダウンロードおよびストリーミング再生ができます。ぜひご利用ください。

Download

Streaming

はじめに

　「英文をしっかり読んで、ゆっくり考えること」を通して、英文に慣れ、英語力を伸ばすことができます。本書は新聞などで報道された英語を用いて、英語力の基礎となる「考える力」を養うテキストです。

　本書の構成は以下の通りです。

Vocabulary Check

　英文記事中の単語の定義を考え、語（句）の意味に迫る問題が 10 問。語（句）について考える機会となります。英文中に出てくる動詞も準動詞（例：現在分詞・過去分詞・不定詞）も定義はすべて to do 〜の形で表しています。

Stream of the Article

　英文全体の「流れをつかむ」+「感じをつかむ」練習です。記事の概要を説明した文などに適切な言葉や文を埋める問題 5 問（a 〜 e）。記事の流れを追って、考えをめぐらせます。

Interpretation and Translation

　記事の中で特に内容や構造的に難解な文の和訳に挑戦する問題 3 問（イロハ）。翻訳を試みることは、内容と構造理解のみならず、日本語表現力も必要で、じっくり考える機会になります。

Grammar and Comprehension

　各 Unit で、理解するのに重要と思われる文法 5 項目に関係した問題 5 問（あ〜お）。問題形式が統一されていないので、しっかりと考える作業が必要になります。

Interpretation and Composition

　各 Unit の記事の内容に関連する、または、重要表現などを使用した英文を作成するための問題 2 問。基本的には英作文ですが、通訳への挑戦も兼ねていて、英語で表現するときに間違いやすい日本語や英語にしにくい日本語表現などに着目します。入念な思考力が求められます。各ジャンルの最初の Unit は、英作文のレベルを基礎的なものにしています。

　本書のコラムには以下の 3 種類があります。

表現の泉

　各 Unit の英文に出てくる単語・表現に関係する言葉に対するコメント、または、表現力を増やすための情報を提供します。

文法の小箱

各 Unit の英文で複雑な構造の文を解説したり、文法の興味深い側面を解説しています。

深堀りの視点

各 Unit のテーマに関する、あまり知られていない事柄について、背景知識を含め、一歩進んだ情報を提供しています。

本書の理念である「考えること」を通して、英語の面白さに気づき、文化・社会・経済・科学の奥深さを知ることができると思います。

本書は、序章、Unit 1、Unit 6、Unit 9、Unit 12、文法問題と文法コラム（文法の小箱）、および巻末の重要単語リスト・重要例文集を石井が、Unit 2 〜 5、Unit 7 〜 8、Unit 10 〜 11、Unit 13 〜 14 の全 10 Unit（文法問題と文法コラムを除く）を喜多が担当しました。

本書を通して、考える力を身につけ、英語力の涵養に少しでも貢献できるのであれば、著者としてこれ以上の喜びはありません。

石井　隆之
喜多　尊史

目次

英文理解を高めるための５つの視点

　ニュース英語の記事を読む前に、英文理解を克服するためには、何に注意する必要があるかを考えてみましょう。５つの視点があります。

①意外な意味

Just as you are **patting yourself on the back for** some big achievement, you run into some unexpected disaster.

　ちょっとした成功を鼻にかけていると思わぬ大失敗をすることになるよ。

　上の例に挙げたように、disaster（大災害）に「大失敗」という意外な意味があります。これに注意しないと意味がわからなくなります。

　たとえば、study に「じっと見る」の意味があるので、Let me study the menu. は、「メニューを見せてください」の意味になります。また、駅員さんに Please produce your ticket. と言われると「切符を拝見します」の意味です。つまり、produce には「（証明のために）見せる」の意味があるのです。

②高度レベルの語法・イディオム

I seem to have lost my get-up-and-go. — When things go wrong from the start, **it's hard to build up momentum**.

　私はどうも張り合いがなくなりましたね。— 出だしからつまずくとは、**ついていないです**ね（←勢いを作り上げるのが難しい）。

　上記の get-up-and-go は「やる気」「覇気」「熱意」の意味。このようなイディオムはたくさん知っていると英文理解力を向上させることになります。

　たとえば、get-out は「（窮地からの）脱出」「回避策」「逃げ口上」などの意味がありますが、as all get-out は口語で「最高に」「極端に」の意味になります。だから It was as hot as all get-out. は「めちゃくちゃ暑かった」の意味です。

③複雑な構造

Insight makes what we read ours.
- （a）直訳＝洞察力は我々が読むものを我々のものにする。
- （b）意訳＝洞察力があれば、読んだものを自分のものにできる。
- （c）翻訳＝洞察力により、読書が自らの血となり肉となる。
- （d）超訳＝生きた読書には洞察力が必要だ。

英文理解力の向上には、①で述べた単語、②で述べたイディオムのほか、着目すべきこと

があります。それは、文法です。複雑な構造が英文理解を難しくしているのですが、文法力があれば、どんな複雑な構造も分析できます。

たとえば、「③に挙げた文の構造は SVOC である」ということが理解できるのは、文法力のなせる業です。

    Insight   makes   what we read   ours.
      S   V   O   C

この構造は、「S は O が C になるよう V する」の基本的な意味を持ちます。だから、直訳すると、上記の（a）のようになります。実際に、この構造を和訳する場合は（b）または、さらに発展させた（c）ぐらいがよいでしょう。

たとえば、次の英文の意味上の微妙な違いがわかりますか。
   （i） John is older than middle-aged.
   （ii） John is more old than middle-aged.
（i）は、「ジョンは中年よりも年を取っている」の意味（「中年を過ぎたぐらい」程度の意味）ですが、（ii）は、「ジョンは『中年』というよりも『年を取っている』と言ったほうがよい」程度の意味です。つまり、（ii）は表現の仕方を問題にしている点で、（i）とは大違いなのです。

このような微妙な差の理解も、文法力があってこそです。

④抽象的内容

At the summit there should be one mind **playing over the whole field**, faithfully aided and corrected but not divided in its integrity.

×summit（山頂）／×mind（心）／×play（遊ぶ）／×field（野原）

首脳会議では、誠意を持って支えられ、間違っていることがあれば正されるのだが、大きな枠組みにおいて（←統合性において［＝ in its integrity］）は、決して迷いはない（←考えが分かれていない［＝ not divided］）ような人が 1 人いて、**全体を見渡している**べきである。

③で述べたように、英文の構造が難しい場合は、理解するのが大変ですが、英文の内容が抽象的であっても、英文理解は難しくなります。

④は単語のレベルの高さとともに、内容の奥深さも手伝って、かなり難しい文となっています。つまり、その英文に出てきた単語の多義性をしっかり理解することも、抽象的な文の理解には役立ちます。summit は「首脳会談」、mind は「人」、play over は「…を見渡す」、field は「分野」であることを理解すれば、上記の英文はほとんど読めていることになります。

⑤専門的内容

What is the greatest whole number such that the sum of 5 and the product of 5 and that whole number is less than 20?

直訳：5 と 5 とあの全体の数の生産物との合計が 20 以下になるような、最も偉大な全体の数は何であるか？

　上記の直訳ではわけがわかりません。ここでの英文理解を阻む要因は、専門的な内容です。これは単に知識がないために英文理解が難しくなるということです。専門家であればちっとも難しいものではありません。上記の英文で、product を数学用語の「積」と考えなければ、何のことだかわかりません。また、whole number は「全体の数」ではなく、数学では「整数」（ちなみに、これは an integral number とか an integer とも表現できます）です。すると、この英文は、次のように分析できるのがわかるでしょう。

　　　the sum of A and B（A と B の和）

　　　the product of C and D（C と D の積）

　　　A ＝ 5、B ＝ the product of 5 and that whole number

　　　C ＝ 5、D ＝ that whole number

　上記のように考えると、⑤の英文は、「5 ＋（5 × D）＜ 20」を満たす最も大きな D は何か？という解釈ができることがわかります。意訳すると以下の通りです。

　意訳：5 と 5 およびある整数の積の和が 20 未満である最大の整数は何か？

　言い換えれば、「不等式 $5 + 5x < 20$」を満たす最大の整数は何か」という問題文であったわけです。ちなみに答えは 2 となります。

　以上、英文理解に必要な視点を 5 つ挙げました。このことを踏まえて、英文を読むと実力が向上するでしょう。応援しています。

1 What is intermittent fasting?
断続的断食とは何か？

🔊 01

① New diets come and go, but a style of eating called "intermittent fasting" has been around for some time now. It became popular after Michael Mosley, a British doctor, wrote a best-selling book in 2012. Intermittent fasting involves switching between periods of eating normally and fasting (or not eating). It's perhaps (あ) [   ] a life-style choice than a diet, as it doesn't tell you what foods to eat — it tells you when to eat.

② The two most common approaches are daily and (い) [   ]: "16:8" is popular for the daily approach. This means you fast for 16 hours each day, and eat during the remaining eight hours. People who prefer the weekly approach generally use "5:2," which Mosley wrote about. (イ) You eat regular meals for five days; for the next two days you limit your food intake to around 600 to 800 calories.

③ Many of us grew up hearing "Eat three regular meals" or "Start your day with a good breakfast." Intermittent fasting (う) [   ] seem to go against traditional ideas about healthy eating. However, humans have actually been fasting for thousands of years. Our ancient ancestors couldn't always find food, so on some days they didn't eat. Many major religions have also used fasting as a spiritual practice.

④ People today eat more food than ever. A report from the United States in 2017 found that the average person was eating 24% more calories than in 1961! We can now buy food at any time of the day, and we stay up late eating snacks while using social media. All this makes it challenging to keep calorie count down.

⑤ (ロ) I tried the 5:2 approach to intermittent fasting some years ago and I found it quite easy to follow. I gradually lost several kilograms over about six months, and successfully maintained my new weight after stopping the 5:2.

⑥ When my children were growing up, we always ate dinner by 7 p.m. Now my children are young adults, however, I can eat when it suits me. I realized I don't feel hungry in the morning. On the other hand, I'm a night owl and go to bed late. Most days, I eat my first meal around 1 to 2 p.m. and then have dinner around 11 p.m., so it is similar to the daily intermittent fasting approach.

⑦ Krista Varady, a professor (え) [   ] the University of Chicago, has researched various styles of eating, including intermittent fasting. "I don't think there's one diet that is better for everyone. The most important thing is finding something that fits into your lifestyle," Varady says. I think most of us can agree with this.

⑧ (ハ) <u>Please note that intermittent fasting isn't recommended for those under 18, pregnant and nursing women, or people with certain health conditions.</u> As with any diet, consult with your doctor before (お) [start / starting / to start].

(July 8, 2022 | Louise George Kittaka - The Japan Times alpha)

---

intermittent 断続的な / approach 方法 / remaining 残りの / ancestor 先祖 / than ever これまでになく、これまで以上に / stay up late 夜遅くまで起きている / fit into one's lifestyle 自らのライフスタイルに合う

Vocabulary Check

定義欄から適切なものを選んで単語の意味・内容を確認しておきましょう。

[単語]

1．around　2．fasting　3．normally　4．intake　5．challenging
6．suit　7．a night owl　8．nutrition　9．nursing　10．consult with

[定義欄]

a. the study of diet and health

b. a person who prefers to be awake and active at night

c. very popular

d. the act of taking something into one's body

e. the act of not eating for some time

f. to seek advice or information from an expert

g. naturally; in a usual way

h. to satisfy someone; to be fitted for someone

i. very difficult; requiring effort but worth doing

j. feeding at the breast

Stream of the Article

　この英文全体を読むと以下のような構成になります。記号（a）から（e）までの内容を記述して、この構成分析を完成させてください。

1．ダイエットの世界はめまぐるしく変化しているが、最近は「断続的断食」が流行している。これは何を食べるかより、（a　　　　　）が重要な新しい方式である。

2．これには2つの一般的方法があり、毎日の方法と毎週の方法である。前者は、毎日16時間断食し、残りの8時間のうちに食べる方式、後者は、（b　　　　　）という方式である。

3．断続的断食は伝統的な健康食の考えに反するように思われるが、過去の人たちは常に食べ物があったわけではなく、また、多くの主要な（c　　　　　）では断食を修行に取り入れている。

4．現代は、過去に比べて食べる量が増えていたり、また、（d　　　　　）するので、摂取カロリーを下げるのは難しい。

5．筆者は、後者の断食をかつてしていたが、現在は、前者のものに近い。いずれにせよ、万人によいダイエットはない、自分に合ったダイエットを見つけること。また、この断続的断食は、18歳以下、妊娠中の女性と（e　　　　　）、あるいは健康状態が悪い人たちにはお勧めできない。

Interpretation and Translation 英➡日

1．②パラグラフの下線部（イ）の意味を日本語で表してください。

_____

_____

2．⑤パラグラフの下線部（ロ）の意味を日本語で表してください。

_____

_____

3．⑧パラグラフの下線部（ハ）の意味を日本語で表してください。

_____

_____

表現の泉

「〇〇学」の英語

第7パラグラフに nutrition（栄養学）が出てきますが、通例、学問名は logy で終わる単語であることが多く、ics や try で終わるものも見られます。

geography（地理学）、geology（地質学）、geometry（幾何学）

biology（生物学）、physics（物理学）、chemistry（化学）

sociology（社会学）、economics（経済学）、linguistics（言語学）

archaeology（考古学）、anthropology（人類学）

otorhinolaryngology（耳鼻咽喉科学）、pediatrics（小児科学）

astrology は過去において「星の学問」でしたが、現在では「占星術」を表し、「天文学」は astronomy となります。

医学の分野の学問名は難しく、日本語では「鳥類学」「魚類学」「蜘蛛学」など漢字で意味がすぐわかるものも、英語では一気に難しくなります。

鳥類学→ ornithology、魚類学→ ichthyology、蜘蛛学→ arachnology

Grammar and Comprehension

1．（あ）の［　　］に入る単語を選んでください。

（A）much　（B）more　（C）most

2．（い）の［　　］に入れるのに最も適切な単語を選んでください。

（A）week　（B）weekly　（C）every week

3．（う）の［　　］に入れるのに最も適切な単語を選んでください。

（A）possible　（B）possibly　（C）ought　（D）might

4．（え）の［　　］に当てはまる語句を選んでください。

（A）at nutrition of　　（B）of nutrition at

（C）with nutrition at　（D）of nutrition with

5．（お）の［　　］の語（句）のうち最も適切なものを選んでください。

［　　　　　　　］

受け身の奥深さ

第 8 パラグラフに "... isn't recommended ..." という受け身の形が出てきますが、すべての SVO の構造において、目的語に意味的な影響がない限り、受け身にはできません。

例 1：I have a book. →✕ A book is had by me.（✕本が私によって持たれている）

「私が本を持っている」ということが、「本」に影響を与えないからです。一方、次の受け身が可能なのは、目的語の cake がなくなるという大きな影響を受けるからです。

例 2：She ate the cake. →〇 The cake was eaten by her.

このことは、〈動詞＋前置詞句〉の構造にも当てはまります。

例 3：〇 The matter was gone into by the scientist.

この文が OK である理由：その件は調べられることにより明らかになる。

✕ The room was gone into by John.

この文が不可である理由：人によって入られたぐらいで部屋は変化しない。

例 4：〇 The chair was sat on by Einstein.

✕ The chair was sat on by me.

例 4 では、前者の chair は付加価値がつくので、受け身が可能なのです。

Interpretation and Composition 🖉 日➡英

次の日本語を英語に訳してください。

1．彼女はまるで友達のみんなが彼女に逆らっているように感じました。

ヒント 〜に逆らっている go against 〜／まるで〜のように感じる feel as if 〜

_____

_____

_____

2．神道と仏教はいろんな点で似ていると思われます。たとえば、両宗教は多神教的であると言えます。

ヒント 〜に似ている similar to 〜／いろんな点で in many ways ／多神教的である polytheistic

_____

_____

_____

深堀りの視点

断食と宗教

　断食とは、一定の期間、自主的に飲食行為をしないことです。医療において検査前の数時間の絶食が必要であるほか、精神保健上の効果（脳内のケトン体の増加による気分の改善・抑うつ）、肥満の解消、デトックス効果などがあると指摘されています。

　断食は、様々な宗教で取り入れられています。紀元前のころから、断食は宗教者の習慣として、『聖書』、『ウパニシャッド』、『クルアーン』（＝コーラン）などで言及されています。

　イスラムにおいては、ラマダン（イスラム暦第 9 月）にて行われる断食が著名ですが、ユダヤ教やキリスト教にも定期的な断食があります。

　ユダヤ教では年 6 回の断食があり、食べ物と水を断ちますが、薬を飲んだり、食べ物のにおいを嗅いだり、歯を磨くことさえも禁止されています。

　キリスト教のいくつかの宗派では、四旬節（復活祭の 40 日前の水曜日［＝灰の水曜日］から復活祭の前日［＝聖土曜日］までの期間）に断食（飲食の節制と祝宴の自粛）が行われます。

　仏教では、「断食は苦行で中道に反する」として推奨されませんが、上座部仏教では正午の食事以降は食事をとりません。これは断食とされず、瞑想を補助する修行の一形態とされています。大乗仏教も、断食は重視しませんが肉食は避けますので、肉を食べない精進料理が編み出されました。

文化

2 Viking-era wooden sailboats make UNESCO's Heritage list
かつての寇船、人類の財産になる！

🎧 02

① For thousands of years, wooden sailboats allowed the peoples of Northern Europe to spread trade, influence and sometimes war across seas and continents. In December, the UN's culture agency added Nordic "clinker boats" to its list of traditions that represent the Intangible Cultural Heritage of Humanity. Denmark, Finland, Iceland, Norway and Sweden jointly sought the UNESCO designation. The term "clinker" is thought (あ) [
] to the way the boat's wooden boards were fastened together.

② (イ) Supporters of the successful nomination hope it will safeguard and preserve the boat-building techniques that drove the Viking era for future generations as the number of people who actively practice the clinker craft fades and fishermen and others opt for vessels with cheaper glass fiber hulls.

③ "We can see that the skills of building them, the skills of sailing the boats, the knowledge of people who are sailing… it goes down and it disappears," said Søren Nielsen, head of boatyard at the Viking Ship Museum in Roskilde, west of Copenhagen. The museum not only exhibits the remains of wooden vessels built 1,000 years ago, but also works to rebuild and reconstruct other Viking boats. The process uses experimental archaeological methods to gain a deeper, (い) [   ] practical understanding of the Viking Age, such as how fast the vessels were and how many people they carried.

④ Nielsen, who oversees the construction and repair of wooden boats built in the clinker tradition, said there are only about 20 people practicing the clinker craft in Denmark, perhaps 200 across all of northern Europe. "We think it's a tradition we have to show off, and we have to tell people (う) this was a part of our background," he told The Associated Press.

⑤ Wooden clinker boats are characterized by the use of overlapping longitudinal wooden hull planks that are sewn or riveted together. Builders (え) [strong] the boats internally by additional wooden components, mainly tall oak trees, which constitute the ribs of the vessel. They stuff the gaps in between with tar or tallow mixed with animal hair, wool and moss.

⑥ "When you build it with these overlaps within it, you get a hull that's quite flexible but at the same time, incredibly strong," explained Triona Sørensen, curator at Roskilde's Viking Ship Museum, which houses the remains of five 11th-century Viking boats built with clinker methods. Nielsen said there is evidence the clinker technique first appeared thousands of years ago, during the Bronze Age.

⑦　But it was during the Viking Age that clinker boats had their zenith, according to Sørensen. (ロ) The era, from 793 to 1066, is when Norse adventurers —Vikings— undertook large-scale voyages, throughout Europe to raid, colonize, conquer and trade throughout Europe. They also reached North America.

⑧　Their light, strong and swift ships were unsurpassed in their time and provided the foundations for kingdoms in Denmark, Norway and Sweden. If "you (お) [　　　　　] any ships, you wouldn't have had any Viking Age, "said Sørensen." It just literally made it possible for them to expand that kind of horizon to become a more global people."

⑨　While the clinker boat tradition in Northern Europe remains to this day, the ships are used by hobbyists, for festivities, regattas and sporting events, rather than raiding and conquest seen 1,000 years ago.

⑩　The UNESCO nomination was signed by around 200 communities and cultural bearers in the field of construction and traditional clinker boat craftsmanship, including Sami communities. (ハ) The inscription on the Intangible Cultural Heritage list obliges the Nordic countries to try to preserve what remains of the fading tradition. "You cannot read how to build a boat in a book, so if you want to be a good boat builder, you have to build a lot of boats," the Viking Ship Museum's Nielsen said. "If you want to keep these skills alive, you have to keep them going."

(February 11, 2022 | The Japan times alpha delivered by AP)

Nordic clinker boats 古代スカンジナビアの鎧張り船 / Intangible Cultural Heritage of Humanity 人類無形文化財 / designation 指定 / remains 遺物 / archeological 考古学の / longitudinal 縦長の / hull planks 船体の厚板 / ribs 肋骨 / tar タール、(たばこの)やに / tallow 獣脂 / moss 苔 / zenith 全盛 / inscription 記載

Vocabulary Check

定義欄から適切なものを選んで単語の意味・内容を確認しておきましょう。

[単語]
　　1．safeguard　2．fade　3．opt for ～　　4．rivet　　5．stuff
　　6．undertake　7．raid　8．unsurpassed　9．festivities　10．regatta

[定義欄]
　a. to set about ～　　　　b. not to be overcome
　c. celebrations　　　　　　d. to attack

e. to protect   f. to make a choice for 〜

g. to fasten with a metal pin h. to fill

i. to disappear   j. boat race

Stream of the Article

この英文全体を読むと以下のような構成になります。ひらがな記号（a）から（e）までの内容を記述して、この構成分析を完成させてください。

１．ヴァイキング船の果たしてきたこと
２．ユネスコ無形文化遺産への登録への動き
３．用語の解説
 具体例：clinker とは（a   ）を意味する。
４．無形文化遺産に登録することの意義
 具体例：登録は（b   ）を保護できる。
５．ヴァイキング船博物館 Nielsen さんの見解
 （1）デンマークでは（c   ）人ほどの人達が clinker 流造船技法を実践している。
 （2）北欧ではこのやり方を行うには 200 名ほどいるであろう。
 （3）これは後世へ伝えるべき技術である。
６．ヴァイキング船の特徴
 具体例：縦の厚板がリベットで打ち付けてある。
 具体例：（d   ）の木が肋骨に使用されている。
７．ヴァイキング時代の（e   ）の説明とヴァイキング船の政治的役割
８．ヴァイキング船の伝統が継承されることへの期待表明

Interpretation and Translation 🖊 英 ➡ 日

１．②パラグラフの下線部（イ）の意味を日本語で表してください。

_____

_____

２．⑦パラグラフの下線部（ロ）の意味を日本語で表してください。

_____

_____

3．⑩パラグラフの下線部（ハ）の意味を日本語で表してください。

_____

_____

表現の泉

characterize の語法

　第5パラグラフの第1文に characterized という単語が出てきます。「Aの特徴はBである」を意味する文の2種類を確認しておきましょう。

　　A is characterized by B.［= B is characteristic of A.］

　例：日本の宗教の特徴は、その神仏習合です。

　　Religions in Japan are characterized by the syncretism of Shinto and Buddhism.

　　The syncretism of Shinto and Buddhism is characteristic of religions in Japan.

Grammar and Comprehension

1．（あ）の［　　］に入れるのに文法的・文脈的に最も適切な形を下から選んでください。
　（A）refer　（B）to refer　（C）referred　（D）referring

2．（い）の［　　］に入れるのに文法的・文脈的に最も適切な形を下から選んでください。
　（A）many　（B）much　（C）more　（D）the more

3．（う）の下線部 this が表すものとして最も適切なものを下から選んでください。
　（A）the construction and repair of wooden boats
　（B）the clinker tradition
　（C）northern Europe
　（D）The Associated Press

4．（え）の［　　］の単語を正しい形にする場合、最も適切なものを下から選んでください。
　（A）stronger　（B）strongly　（C）strength　（D）strengthen

5．（お）の［　　］に入れるのに文法的に最も適切な形を下から選んでください。
　（A）not have　（B）didn't have　（C）hadn't had　（D）wouldn't have had

関係代名詞の省略の真実

第4パラグラフに a tradition we have to show off がありますが、これは tradition（先行詞）の直後の関係代名詞目的格（which または that）が省略されています。

一般に、関係代名詞の目的格は省略できます。

例1：the book that I bought →○ the book I bought

ところが、関係代名詞の直後に主語が来ない場合は省略ができません。

例2：the truth that probably the man hid（恐らくその男が隠した真実）

　　　→× the truth probably the man hid

主格であっても省略できる場合があります。

例3：the animal which I think is on the verge of extinction

　　　→○ the animal I think is on the verge of extinction（絶滅危惧種と思う動物）

また、非制限用法の場合は、目的格であっても省略は不可能です。

例4：John, whom Mary loves（メアリーが愛しているジョン）

　　　→× John, Mary loves

つまり、関係代名詞の省略について次の法則が成り立つと言えます。

法則：「先行詞＋関係代名詞＋主語＋動詞」の連続において関係代名詞は省略できる

例4が不可なのは、「先行詞＋コンマ＋関係代名詞＋主語＋動詞」の構造だからです。

なお、例4が文として成立する場合は、話題化構文と言い、「O，SV」の構造で、目的語が話題化されて、「OはSがVする」を意味することになります。

John, Mary loves.（ジョンはメアリーが愛している）

Interpretation and Composition 🖊 日 ➡ 英

以下の日本語をよく読んで、下線部のみを通訳してください。

1. ヴァイキング船はイングランド沿岸も略奪してまわった。しかし書籍は邪魔で捨てるかあるいは燃やして暖をとったのだろう。古英語の時代の貴重な文献がかなり失われた。逆説めくが「もう二度と手に入らない」という状態になったからこそ、英国で古学が芽生え始めた。カトリックの修道院などでは残った本を大事に「蒐集」し「修理」して「分類」し始めたのである。

ヒント 古英語 Old English ／文献 books and documents ／古学 study of antiquities

2. 日本では織豊政権末期の頃の話だが、英国にはフランシス・ドレークという男がいた。英国海軍のご先祖のような人だ。プリマスの投資家たちが金を出し応援した。ドレーク（1596 年没）と荒くれ男どもは南米チリからスペインに向かう商船を襲い 2 万ポンドほどの貴金属を奪い取った。彼はしばしば略奪品の多くを女王エリザベス一世に献じたところ、お褒めのことばを賜り、後には貴族に叙せられている。

> **ヒント** フランシス・ドレーク Francis Drake（d.1596）／貴金属 precious metals ／略奪品 loot, plunder ／貴族に叙する to dub 〜 a knight

---

深堀りの視点

日英歴史対比

　紀元 800 年前半（829 年説も）以来ヴァイキングの襲撃はブリテン島の住民を苦しめます。アルフレッド大王治政下（871 〜 899 年）、一時的に侵略を食い止め部分的には撃退に成功しますが、ついには 1016 年にヴァイキング勢力がこの島を支配することになりました（デーン王朝）。1042 年にはこの島は再びアングロサクソンの支配する政治形態に戻りますが、その後、1066 年にノルマン王朝（フランス人の支配）がブリテン島に成立しておよそ 300 年間続きました。つまり、ブリテン島は外国からの脅威にさらされ続けてついに外国の占領下に置かれたということになります。

　ヴァイキングの強さは「いつどこに現れるかわからない」という神出鬼没性にあります。これは防御する側には大きな負担になります。Speed and Mobility を兼ね備えていましたので、守勢に立つ側は防ぎようがありませんでした。この特徴は現代において潜水艦に受け継がれています。

　さて、ブリテン島民が塗炭の苦しみに喘ぐその時期、日本では平安時代でした。坂上田村麻呂の蝦夷征伐（801 年）があり、最澄と空海は遣唐使に従い入唐（804 年）していました。内政では人臣最初の摂政職（858 年）と（初めての）関白職（884 年）を藤原氏が独占する時期が続きました。承和の変（842 年）や応天門の変（866 年）などがあったものの外国勢力による王朝の交代などはありませんでした。また、894 年には菅原道真の献言により遣唐使を廃止して内政の充実に努めました。

　900 年に入ると「延喜（901 〜 923 年）・天暦の治（947 〜 957 年）」といわれる時期に入り、醍醐天皇が理想的な政治を行ったとされています。政治的安定はさらに続き、村上天皇が理想的な政治を引き継ぎました。とくに、醍醐天皇は摂政も関白も太政大臣も置かずに親政を行ったとされています。

文化

3 Nigeria town celebrates claim as "twin's capital" of world
ママの食べ物で決まるのか？

① The sign greeting visitors at the entrance of Igbo-Ora in southwest Nigeria welcomes people to "TWINS CAPITAL OF THE WORLD".

② The sleepy-looking town boasts of having the highest concentration of multiple births of any place on the globe.

③ (イ) To celebrate its self-proclaimed title the town hosts an annual festival, now in its second year, that draws hundreds of sets of twins from around the country.

④ Donning different traditional clothes and costumes, the twins — male and female, old, young and even newborn — sang and danced at the latest edition last month to the appreciation of an admiring audience.

⑤ "We feel elated that we are being honored today," Kehinde Durowoju, a 40-year-old twin, said as he hugged his identical brother Taiwo.

⑥ "With this event, the whole world will better appreciate the importance of Ibeji (twins) as special children and gifts from God."

⑦ Around them, twins moved in procession to show off their colorful outfits as magic displays and masquerades also entertained the crowds.

⑧ Population experts say the Yoruba-speaking southwest has one of the highest twinning rates in Nigeria.

⑨ Statistics (あ) [   ] to come by, but a study by British gynecologist Patrick Nylander, between 1972 and 1982, recorded an average of 45 to 50 sets of twins per 1,000 live births in the region.

⑩ That compares to a twin birth rate of 33 per every 1,000 births in the United States, according to the National Center for Health Statistics.

⑪ Igbo-Ora is the epicenter of the phenomenon in the West African country.

⑫ Residents in the town, some 100 kilometers north of Nigeria's biggest city, Lagos, say that almost every family has some twins.

⑬ Traditional leader Jimoh Olajide Titiloye knows all about this special quirk.

⑭ "I am a twin, my wife is a twin and I have twins as children," he said.

⑮ (ロ) "There is hardly any household in this town which does not have at least a set of twins."

⑯　He said the festival on Oct.19 was aimed at promoting Igbo-Ora as "the foremost twins tourism destination in the world" and (い) [if / that / which / whose] efforts were underway to get the town listed in the Guinness Book of Records.

⑰　Prominent Yoruba ruler, the Alaafin of Oyo, Oba Lamidi Adeyemi, said the festival "is a celebration of culture and recognition of Ibeji as special children in Yorubaland".

⑱　He said the birth of twins usually "heralds peace, progress, prosperity and good luck to their parents," adding that parents should always take good care of them.

⑲　But while twins are seen as a blessing by many today, that has not always been the case in parts of southern Nigeria.

⑳　In pre-colonial times twins were often regarded as evil and were (う) [　　　　　] banished to the "evil forest" or killed.

㉑　(ハ) Scottish missionary Mary Slessor is widely credited with helping to curb the practice in the late 19th century.

㉒　Scientists have not said definitively why Igbo-Ora has such a high number of twins.

㉓　Local residents have a theory that it is down to the diet of women in the town.

㉔　"Our people eat okra leaf or Ilasa soup with yam and amala (cassava flour)," community leader Samuel Adewuyi Adeleye said.

㉕　(え) [　　　　　　　　]

㉖　"The water we drink also contributes to the phenomenon," Adeleye added.

㉗　Fertility experts are skeptical — and point to another explanation.

㉘　They say there is (お) [no / not] proven link between diet and the high birth rate, with the same food being consumed across the region.

㉙　"It's a genetic thing," said Emmanuel Akinyemi, the medical director of Lagos-based Estate Clinic.

㉚　"I think the gene for multiple births is in the region and this has been passed on from generation to generation."　　(November 8, 2019 | The Japan times alpha delivered by AFP-JIJI)

---

multiple births 多胎出産 / at the latest edition last month つい先月のお祭りに参加して（←意訳「（祭りの）最新版」）/ to the appreciation of an admiring audience すっかり感心している聴衆が価値を認めてくれるので / identical (brother) 一卵性双生児の（兄弟）/ masquerade 仮装、仮面舞踏会 / gynecologist 婦人科医 / this special quirk 不思議な現象 / Yoruba ヨルバ人 / Alaafin of Oyo オヨ王国の王 [alaafin は「王」の意味]（オヨ王国は1400年ごろから1905年まで、ナイジェリア南東部を支配したヨルバ人の王国）/ okra leaf オクラ（アオイ科の植物）/ yam ヤマノイモ / cassava キャッサバでんぷん（タピオカの原料）/ fertility expert 生殖の専門家

Vocabulary Check

定義欄から適切なものを選んで単語の意味・内容を確認しておきましょう。

[単語]

1．self-proclaimed　2．don　3．feel elated　4．come by 〜　5．epicenter
6．herald　7．banish to 〜　8．be credited with helping 〜　9．curb
10．be down to 〜

[定義欄]

a. to put 〜 on or to wear　　　b. the central point

c. announced by oneself　　　d. to announce

e. to feel very happy　　　f. to suppress; to check

g. to be believed to have helped 〜　h. to give up or send to 〜

i. to result from　　　j. to obtain

Stream of the Article

　この英文全体を読むと以下のような構成になります。記号（a）から（e）までの内容を記述して、この構成分析を完成させてください。

1．双子の町 Igbo-Ora の紹介
2．この土地では双子が生まれる率が高い。
3．双子の祭りの様子の紹介
　　具体例：（a　　　　）を身につけて双子の（老若男女）たちが歌い踊る。
4．人口調査の専門家の意見
5．英国人（b　　　　）科の医師 Patrick Nylander 氏が 1972-1982 年までに行った調査の結果紹介
6．Igbo-Ora の住人の意見や実態を紹介
7．双子の意味と親の責任について
8．双子の扱い方の変遷について
　　具体例：植民地になる前の時代には双子は（c　　　　）されるか殺されていた。
9．科学者の見解について
10．地元の人は双子の多い理由を「女性の（d　　　　）」にあると述べている。
11．食事の内容を紹介
12．生殖専門家は「双子と食事の関係」は（e　　　　）的な見解だ。
13．遺伝的要因説の紹介

Interpretation and Translation 🖉 英➡日

1．③パラグラフの下線部（イ）の意味を日本語で表してください。

_____

_____

2．⑮パラグラフの下線部（ロ）の意味を日本語で表してください。

_____

_____

3．㉑パラグラフの下線部（ハ）の意味を日本語で表してください。

_____

_____

表現の泉

Fratricide（兄弟殺し）

　兄弟がいれば必ず喧嘩が生じ、それが時に殺人にまで至る場合もあります。アダムとイブの子供たちカインとアベルにも争いがありました。

　And the Lord said unto Cain, "Where is Abel thy brother?" (Genesis 4:9 ～ 10)

　この場面は旧約聖書の創世記にあります。カイン（Cain）が弟を殺害した後での問答。「弟アベル（Abel）はどこにいるのか」と Lord（神）は問います。Cain はどのように答えたのでしょうか？ He said, "I do not know; am I my brother's keeper?"

　カインは「私は弟の番人でしょうか？」と答えましたが、"What have you done?" と Lord（神）はさらに追及します。

　この Am I my brother's keeper? は少し形を変えた種々の場面でも使われています。たとえば否定形（I am not my brother's keeper）で使えば「知るものか」という感じも出てきます。また my brother's keeper を his keeper とすれば「あいつのことなど知らない」という意味になります。

Grammar and Comprehension

1. （あ）の [   ] に入れるのに文法的・文脈的に正しい語句を下から選んでください。

   （A）is important　（B）are important　（C）is difficult　（D）are difficult

2. （い）の [   ] 内の単語のうち正しいものを選んでください。

   [   ]

3. （う）の [   ] に入れるのに文法的・文脈的に正しい単語を下から選んでください。

   （A）not　（B）either　（C）neither　（D）both

4. （え）の [   ] に入れるのに文法的・文脈的に正しい文を下から選んでください。

   （A）Gonadotropins, a chemical substance that helps women to produce multiple eggs, are believing that it contains yams.

   （B）Women are believed to contain gonadotropins, a chemical substance that helps yams to produce multiple eggs.

   （C）Yams are believed to contain gonadotropins, a chemical substance that helps women to produce multiple eggs.

   （D）Multiple eggs are to believe containing gonadotropins, a chemical substance that helps women to produce yams.

5. （お）の [   ] 内の単語のうち正しいほうを選んでください。

   [   ]

文法の小箱

構造の理解

　第8パラグラフの文、Population experts say the Yoruba-speaking southwest has one of the highest twinning rates in Nigeria. について解説します。

　〈目的語（O）＋ハイフン＋動詞（V）ing〉で「OをVする」という意味の形容詞を作り、〈動詞（V）ing＋名詞（N）〉で「VするN」という意味の名詞を作ります。従って、Yoruba-speaking は「ヨルバ語を話す」、twinning rates は「双子を生む比率」（twin に「双子を産む」という動詞の用法がある）という意味になります。

　よって、この文の試訳は「人口の専門家によると、ヨルバ語を話す南西部は、ナイジェリアでは最も高い双子出生率を有する一地域となっている。」となります。「one of the 最上級」の形を意識し、意訳しています。

Interpretation and Composition 🖊 日 ➡ 英

　以下の日本語をよく読んで、下線部のみを通訳してください。

1．双子という表現が時には「よく似た」という意味を含むことがある。ところで日本の外交にも類似したことが何度か起こっている。「大事なときに大使が失敗する」という不名誉な類似性だ。たとえば湾岸危機（1990 年 8 月）時には在イラク大使も在クエート大使も任地にはいなかった。ソ連のクーデター（1991 年 8 月）のときも駐ソ大使はモスクワに不在だった。

　　🔵ヒント 外交 diplomacy ／不名誉な dishonorable, disgraceful

_____

_____

_____

2．日米開戦のときにも駐米大使は取り返しのつかないことをした。開戦の通告を予定時刻にハル国務長官に手渡すことができずに「ハワイのだまし討ち」の汚名を歴史に刻んだ。前の晩にやるべき暗号解読とそのタイプ打ちを済ませていなかったからだというのだ。

　　🔵ヒント 開戦の通告 declare war ／だまし討ち sneak attack ／暗号解読 break the code, codebreaking

_____

_____

_____

深堀りの視点

多胎児

　同じ母親の胎内で同時期に発育して生まれた複数の子供を多胎児と呼びます。日本語で多胎児は双生児を含みます。英語では、双生児は twins、三つ子以上は supertwins と言います。

　日本では、後から生まれた子を兄（or 姉）という風習がありましたが、1874 年 12 月 13 日の太政官指令により、生まれた順に兄弟姉妹が定まるようになりました。先に生まれたら、兄（or 姉）となったのです。

　胎児が 2 人は双胎（=twins）、3 人は品胎（= triplets）、4 人は要胎（= quadruplets）、5 人は周胎（= quintuplets）と言います。3・4・5 人を表す漢字（品・要・周）は、その漢字が持つ□の（四角のような）空間の数を胎児の数に見立てたものです。

4 Artist adorns Egyptian cave church with biblical art
岩窟教会に聖書の世界を刻む男がいる！

🔊 04

① (イ) Whistling a tune, Mario nimbly clambered up the scaffolding enveloping part of the rock-hewn St. Simon Monastery atop Cairo's Mokkatam hills to add the final touches to his latest sculpture.

② He had spent more than two decades carving the rugged insides of the seven cave churches and chapels of the monastery with designs inspired by biblical stories.

③ It was all done to fulfil the wishes of the monastery's parish priest who met Mario in the early 1990s in Cairo. The Polish artist, who had arrived in Egypt earlier on an educational mission, was then looking for an opportunity to serve God at the monastery.

④ " (あ) [　　　　　] to turn the mountain into an open Bible," Mario recalls the priest telling him.

⑤ Back then, Mario had no experience in sculpting. But he bought an electric drill and chisel hammer and within days had finished his first sculpture.

⑥ It told the story of the miracle of the moving of Mokkatam mountain, (い) a feat said to have been done by a 10th century craftsman known as Simon the Tanner to prove the strength of his Christian faith. The monastery is named after him.

⑦ (ロ) "I had no idea sculpting was a talent I have, but it turned out (to be) as you can see," said Mario as he showed off his work around the walls of a vast cavern which regularly hosts gatherings at the monastery.

⑧ Across (う) one, he sketched another chronicle about St. Simon, shown brandishing a needle before gouging his eyes out to punish himself for lusting after a woman.

⑨ Other walls recount stories from the New Testament.

⑩ "My work is meant to tell spiritual stories of this mountain and of Christianity in general," he said. "I want them to live on for future generations."

⑪ Mario says he kept practicing, sculpting for more than 23 years, and completed about 70 sculptures adding to the monastery's allure by giving it an ancient look.

⑫ Construction of the complex started only in the 1970s, a thousand years after the story of moving Mokkatam mountain believed to have taken place in November, 979.

⑬ Building began after the monastery's current parish priest known as Father Samaan, Arabic for Simon, visited the area and decided to turn it into a worship place.

⑭ "I also thought then why not carve the miracles of Jesus on the mountain. It will benefit the people and (create) a lively depiction of these stories," said Father Samaan.

⑮ Resting at the pinnacle of Mokkatam mountain, the monastery has a commanding view of the megalopolis of Cairo. Unsurprisingly though, reaching the top of the mountain is no small feat.

⑯ The gruelling trip to the top requires visitors to pass through the teeming slum area known as the city of "Garbage Collectors" of uneven roads and malodorous piles of garbage strewn along the way.

⑰ Despite the tough journey, the monastery welcomes thousands for services weekly as well as on holidays and celebrations of the Copts, Egypt's Christian minority which makes up about 10 percent of the country's Muslim-majority population.

⑱ "The monastery is now a masterpiece," Samaan said in his office in one of the churches of the monastery. "We have the pyramids and the artefacts in the Egyptian museum. But they are all ancient but this monastery is new."

⑲ Mario, whose real name is Mariusz Dybich, said he has grown accustomed to life in Cairo and work at the monastery.

⑳ (え) [   ] is originally from the city of Krakow in southern Poland but has been living in Egypt for nearly three decades now. He has over the years become known to everyone in the monastery and the thousands of people living in the city of "Garbage Collectors" by his nickname, Mario.

㉑ (ハ) He married an Egyptian woman and has two girls. He mastered over the years the Arabic language and developed a particularly strong command of the Egyptian dialect.

㉒ In 2011, Mario witnessed the uprising that toppled longtime autocrat Hosni Mubarak and led to years of political and economic turmoil.

㉓ Yet Mario does not see himself settling anywhere else.

㉔ "I just love living here. It's where I am (お) [most / the most] comfortable - among the simple people of Egypt. I would not leave unless God decides otherwise."

(August 16, 2019 | The Japan times alpha delivered by AFP-JIJI)

---

scaffolding 足場 / feat 偉大な業績 / cavern 岩窟 / brandish （刀などを）振り回す / lusting 欲情 / allure 魅力 / pinnacle 頂上 / autocrat 独裁者 / turmoil 混乱

Vocabulary Check

定義欄から適切なものを選んで単語の意味・内容を確認しておきましょう。

[単語]

    1．nimbly 2．clamber up 3．rock-hewn   4．rugged   5．brandish

6．gouge　7．gruelling　　8．malodorous　9．the Copts　10．topple

［定義欄］
a. made by cutting rock　　　b. exhausting

c. quickly　　　　　　　　　d. to remove 〜 out

e. to climb up 〜 with difficulty　f. producing an unpleasant smell

g. a Christian ethnoreligious group native to North Africa

h. to wave around 〜　　　　i. to make 〜 lose power

j. not smooth or flat

Stream of the Article

　この英文全体を読むと以下のような構成になります。記号（a）から（e）までの内容を記述して、この構成分析を完成させてください。

1．岩窟彫刻家マリオと岩窟教会の紹介

2．マリオと教区司祭の出会いについて

3．主任司祭は「（a　　　　）をしてもらいたい」とマリオに述べた。

4．マリオには（b　　　　）としての経験がなかった。

5．聖シモンが自分の目をえぐり出す場面

6．新約聖書の場面を扱った壁面もある。

7．979 年に信仰の力で（c　　　　）を動かした場面

8．この教会のある教区を現在担当する神父の名前は（d　　　　）という。

9．この神父は「イエスの奇跡の場面も彫刻してもらいたい」と希望している。

10．この教会にたどり着くにはスラム街を通り抜ける必要がある。

11．この教会には数多くの人が週末や休みには訪れる。

12．この教会では少数派教徒の（e　　　　）信者も受け入れている。

13．マリオはエジプトに住んですでに 30 年ほどになる。

Interpretation and Translation　英➡日

1．①パラグラフの下線部（イ）の意味を日本語で表してください。

_____

_____

２．⑦パラグラフの下線部（ロ）の意味を日本語で表してください。

_____

_____

３．㉑パラグラフの下線部（ハ）の意味を日本語で表してください。

_____

_____

表現の泉

綴りの似た単語

　第8パラグラフ2行目に gouge という単語の ing 形が出てきましたが、この単語の綴りとよく似た綴りの単語があります。注意しましょう。

gouge [gáudʒ] えぐる
　　　Some meteorites gouge out huge craters.
　　　隕石の中には巨大なクレーターをつくるものがある。

gauge [géidʒ] 規格、標準、寸法
　　　Popularity is rarely a true gauge of one's ability.
　　　人気があるということが能力の真の基準になることは稀である。

gorge [gɔ́:rdʒ] たらふく食べる
　　　The girls gorged themselves on cake at the party.
　　　少女たちはそのパーティでケーキをいっぱい食べた。

Grammar and Comprehension

１．（あ）にはどの語句を入れると意味が合いますか。正しい語句を選んでください。
　　（A）You want me　（B）I want you　（C）He wants me　（D）I want him

２．（い）の下線部を、どのように書き換えることができますか。正しいものを下から選んでください。
　　（A）a feat said it to have been done　　（B）a feat that was said to be done
　　（C）a feat that is said to have been done　（D）a feat is said to have done

３．（う）の one が表しているものを選んでください。
　　（A）One of the walls　（B）A vast cavern
　　（C）Mario's work　　（D）A certain gathering

4．（え）の［　　　］に入れるのに最も適切な語句を選んでください。

　　（A）A 51-year-old　（B）A 51-years-old　（C）The 51-year-old　（D）The 51-years-old

5．（お）の［　　　］の2つの表現のうち正しいほうを選んでください。［　　　　　　　　　］

文法の小箱

構造の理解

　第17パラグラフを構成する文の構造を解説します。Despite the tough journey, the monastery welcomes thousands for services weekly as well as on holidays and celebrations of the Copts, Egypt's Christian minority which makes up about 10 percent of the country's Muslim-majority population. において、the Copts の直後のコンマは、同格を表し、これが Egypt's 以下と同じであることを意味します。従って、Egypt's ... は Copts の説明となります。

　A as well as B（＝ B だけでなく A）の構造において、A=weekly、B=on holidays and celebrations of the Copts となります。which の先行詞は、Egypt's Christian minority です。

　この文の試訳は「そこへ至るのに厳しい道のりですが、その修道院は、コプトの祝日や祝祭のときだけでなく、毎週1回、ミサのために何千人もの人たちを受け入れています。コプトとは、イスラム教徒が大半であるエジプトの人口の約10%を占める、少数派のキリスト教徒です。」となります。

Interpretation and Composition 　🖊 日➡英

以下の日本語をよく読んで、下線部のみを通訳してください。

1．仏教寺院に極楽浄土の様子が描かれたり彫刻されたりしていても、変だとは思わないだろう。ところで極楽も地獄もないと教える仏教の一派もある。では、極楽や地獄の様子を描いた絵はいったい何であろう。魂などないという前提に立つ宗派もある。するとたちまち困ることが起きる。何が輪廻転生するのか？という難問が出てくるからだ。

　ヒント 一派 sect, group ／前提 assumption, assuming that ～／輪廻転生 reincarnation, rebirth of the soul into another body

---

2．そのような疑問や矛盾に関係なく仏画は描かれてきたし、これからも仏像は彫刻され続けるだろう。さらには日本では仏教用語や習慣がありふれている。そのために何となく仏教がわかった気になるのだが、実は仏教の教義は難解至極であり、経典もわからなくて当然だ。仕方なくインドの説話を助けとして用いているが、これにはヒンズー教の思想も入り込んでいて、逆に仏教理解を妨げているらしい。

ヒント 教義 teaching, belief ／経典 Sutra, Holy Scripture ／ヒンズー教 Hinduism

---

深掘りの視点

奇跡とカリスマ

　新約聖書「ルカによる福音書」にはイエスによる奇跡を起こす能力の実例とその能力の伝授が記されています。ルカ（10:17-20）「さて72人（の弟子）は喜びを抱いて帰ってきた」という記述がありますが、これは弟子たちが悪魔を服従させた話です。

　これとは別に、ルカ（9:1-3）にはイエスが12使徒に病気を治す能力と悪魔祓いの権威を授与する場面が出てきます。奇跡の能力は弟子たちも（授けてもらい）持っていたことがわかります。

　さらには、ルカ（9:49-50）には「先生、あなたのみ名によって悪魔を追い出している人を私たちは見ました」と記されていますが、この人はイエス教団に従っている人ではなかったとも記されています。これらの記述からもイエスとその弟子たち以外にも悪魔祓いのできる人がいたことがわかります。

　イエスとほぼ同時代の人であり不思議な遠隔治療を行ったとされる人物がいます。ハニナ・ベン・ドーザという人です。この人物は伝道者パウロの師（ガマリエル）の息子を助けましたが、その折に遠隔除霊か遠隔治癒の能力を使ったと伝えられています。

5 Floating fortress Musashi, symbol of Japan's naval ambitions, now a war grave
戦艦武蔵発見、戦没者の御霊安らかに

◀| 05

① The super-dreadnought that once served as the flagship of the Imperial Japanese Navy has been found lying in sections in the dark ocean depths of the Philippines, 70 years after the end of World War II.

② Billionaire Microsoft co-founder Paul Allen announced on March 3 that his research team located the wreck of the Musashi, one of the two largest and most technologically advanced battleships in naval history, 1,000 meters below the surface of the Sibuyan Sea.

③ (イ) The news immediately made headlines in Japan, with video clips and photos taken by a remotely operated undersea vehicle repeatedly aired on television, drawing reactions of awe and surprise.

④ But what was the Musashi? What made the warship so special? Why was such a formidable vessel built and how did it meet its end?

⑤ Following are some questions and answers about the Musashi, a symbol of Japan's advanced engineering capabilities, the nation's tragedies and a colossal failure in war strategy that made the vessel obsolete before it even set sail: What was the Musashi?

⑥ It was one of two Yamato-class battleships of the Imperial navy, (あ) [   ] the Yamato, and was also one of the world's largest and most powerful ever built.

⑦ (い) [   ] in 1942, the Musashi was the last battleship Japan built. Its predecessor, the Yamato, was commissioned on Dec. 16, 1941, just days after Japan attacked Pearl Harbor to start the Pacific War.

⑧ The Musashi, which was commissioned on Aug. 5, 1942, became the flagship of Japan's main fleet on Feb. 11, 1943, following the Yamato.

⑨ Both the Musashi and Yamato displaced 64,000 tons. Their 46-cm main guns were the largest and most powerful ever to be mounted on a warship.

⑩ The two ships, each capable of carrying six reconnaissance aircraft, were 263 meters long. (The diameter of Tokyo Dome is 201 meters.)

⑪ The ships had a maximum height of 56 meters, about the same as a 16-story building, and could reach a maximum cruising speed of 50 kph.

⑫ The main guns could lob a 1½-ton shell 42 km, meaning a round fired from Tokyo

Tower in Minato Ward could reach Kamakura Station in Kanagawa Prefecture.

⑬　The existence and specifications of the Musashi and Yamato, in particular those of the main guns, were designated top military secrets. Why were such mammoth battleships planned in the first place?

⑭　Before World War II, it was generally believed (う) [having / to have] large warships with long-range guns offered a critical military advantage in naval warfare.

⑮　Naval air power was still in its early stages and carrier aircraft (え) [was / were] not believed capable of sinking a large, heavily armored battleship.

⑯　(ロ) The Imperial Japanese Navy in particular turned to size and powerful guns because of the 1922 Washington Naval Treaty and 1930 London Naval Treaty, which allowed Japan, a rising power and perceived threat, in the Pacific to possess much fewer major warships than the United States, its main hypothetical naval foe at the time. Did the Musashi and Yamato contribute greatly to Japan's war effort?

⑰　Not really. The Imperial navy, which considered both vessels symbols of Japan's naval prowess, was initially reluctant to deploy the ships to major battle zones.

⑱　(ハ) The two battleships, with elite commanders, stayed safe in port at the Truck Islands (now Chuuk Islands) until spring 1944. While idle, they were dubbed "Inn Musashi" and "Hotel Yamato," given their well-appointed interiors and lavish meals for elite officers.

⑲　Only after Japan lost its main aircraft carriers and numerous skilled pilots in the 1942 Battle of Midway and the 1944 Battle of the Philippine Sea, and other battles started to go against the country, (お) [　　　　　　　] to put the two battleships in harm's way.

⑳　Lacking the protection of fighter planes, the Musashi was sunk on Oct. 24, 1944, after being hit by an estimated 20 to 30 torpedoes and 17 bombs from enemy aircraft.

㉑　Of the 2,400 or so crew members aboard the Musashi, only 1,376 reportedly survived the battle. The Yamato, later dispatched on a suicide mission at the start of the Battle of Okinawa, was sunk by U.S. forces on April 7, 1945, off Kagoshima Prefecture.

㉒　Were the Yamato-type battleships the products of flawed strategic thinking?

㉓　Yes. Large, heavily armored battleships were designed for surface warfare, based on the concept that they could not be sunk by aircraft.

㉔　World War II, particularly in the Pacific, saw the ascent of the concept of naval air superiority. Long-range land-based warplanes also doomed the battleship.

㉕　When the Yamato-class ships were designed, it wasn't thought possible that aircraft could deliver the powerful bombs and torpedoes needed to sink them, according to "Senkan Musashi Kenzo Kiroku" ("Construction of The Musashi"), published in 1994.

㉖　When the Imperial navy realized the threat of air power, it initially only sought to deploy the Musashi and Yamato to locations where Japan maintained air superiority.

㉗　The designers had assumed the Musashi would be at risk from torpedoes launched by enemy ships and submarines, but not airplanes, the book said.

㉘ Ironically, it was the Imperial navy that first demonstrated to the world that carrier aircraft, not battleships, would be the key to prevailing in naval warfare during World War II.

㉙ Japan, which for a while had the most modern and largest aircraft carrier fleet, demonstrated its naval air power with the Pearl Harbor attack on Dec. 7, 1941 (Dec. 8 in Japan).

㉚ Two days later, Japanese aircraft again shocked the world by sinking Britain's powerful battleship the Prince of Wales and battle cruiser Repulse off the Malay Peninsula.

㉛ Today's military experts say the sinking of the Prince of Wales marked the end of the era of huge battleships in naval warfare.

(March 16, 2015 | The Japan Times)

super-dreadnought 超弩級（の戦艦）/ video clip 短いビデオ映像 / obsolete 老朽化した / flagship 旗艦 / displace 〜の排水量である / reconnaissance aircraft 偵察機 / lob 弧を描くように高く打ち上げる / a round 砲弾 / specification 性能 / carrier aircraft 航空母艦 / Washington Naval Treaty ワシントン海軍軍縮会議 / London Naval Treaty ロンドン海軍軍縮会議 / Chuuk Islands チューク諸島 / put 〜 in harm's way 〜を危険な状況に晒す / flawed strategic thinking 根本的に誤った戦略思想 / aircraft carrier fleet 空母部隊 / cruiser 巡洋艦

Vocabulary check

定義欄から適切なものを選んで単語の意味・内容を確認しておきましょう。

[単語]

1．wreck　　2．air　　3．formidable　4．commissioned　5．critical
6．hypothetical　7．lavish　8．doom　　9．deploy　　10．prevailing

[定義欄]

a. to broadcast

b. to condemn 〜 to death

c. decisive

d. emerging victorious

e. brought into working condition

f. to move 〜 into position for military action

g. a destroyed ship

h. supposed

i. elaborate or luxurious

j. inspiring fear and awe

Stream of the Article

　この英文全体を読むと以下のような構成になります。記号（a）から（e）までの内容を記述して、この構成分析を完成させてください。

1. 日本海軍の戦艦武蔵の発見
2. 海底 1,000 メートルに横たわる武蔵
3. 発見時の戦艦の状態は（a　　　　）だった。
4. 武蔵発見のニュースは世界をかけめぐった。
5. 武蔵は日本海軍主力艦隊の（b　　　　）になった。
6. 当時は武蔵の性能その他は極秘扱い。
7. 二つの軍縮会議の結果、日本海軍は大艦巨砲に勝機を見出すようになった。
8. 当初、大和・武蔵は（c　　　　）に投入されなかった。
9. 航空戦力の不足から 1944 年 10 月 24 日沈没。
10. 戦略的思想に誤りがあった？
11. 敵の航空戦力が予想を超えて強力になった。
12. 武蔵の建造時には（d　　　　）からの魚雷攻撃は想定していなかった。
13. しかし空母搭載機の実力を初めて世界に示したのは皮肉なことに（e　　　　）であった。　例：ハワイ作戦、マレー半島沖の海戦

Interpretation and Translation 🖊 英➡日

1. ③パラグラフの下線部（イ）の意味を日本語で表してください。

_____

_____

2. ⑯パラグラフの下線部（ロ）の意味を日本語で表してください。

_____

_____

3. ⑱パラグラフの下線部（ハ）の意味を日本語で表してください。

_____

_____

船舶および艦船関連の表現

新聞や雑誌に軍事記事が掲載されるときがあります。そのような場合に艦船単語を知らないと困ります。以下に掲載するのはおなじみの船舶・艦船用語です。

starboard 右舷・面舵 → Hard to starboard! 面舵いっぱい =Right full rudder!

port 左舷・取り舵 → Hard to port! 取り舵いっぱい =Left full rudder!

bow 船首　stern 船尾　hull 船体

deck 甲板 → main deck 正甲板 / quarter deck 後甲板 / flight deck (flying deck) 飛行甲板

bridge 艦橋 → flying bridge 最高艦橋

main battery 主砲　secondary battery 副砲　antiaircraft gun 高角砲（対空砲）

caliber (bore) 口径 → a gun of 18-inch caliber 18インチ砲

propeller スクリュー　rudder 舵　con 操舵する

sail 潜水艦の司令塔　periscope 潜望鏡

torpedo 魚雷 → launch a torpedo 魚雷を発射する

dive 潜航する　surface 浮上する

Grammar and Comprehension

1．（あ）の［　　　］に入れるのに文法的・文脈的に正しい語句を選んでください。

　（A）another was　　（B）another being

　（C）the other was　　（D）the other being

2．（い）の［　　　］に入れるのに文法的に正しい単語を選んでください。

　（A）Build　（B）To build　（C）Built　（D）Building

3．（う）の［　　　］内の単語のうち全体の文が文法的に正しくなるものを選んでください。
　［　　　　　　　］

4．（え）の［　　　］内の単語のうち全体の文が文法的に正しくなるものを選んでください。
　［　　　　　　　］

5．（お）の［　　　］に入れるのに文法的・文脈的に正しい語句を選んでください。

　（A）the navy started　（B）did the navy start

　（C）started the navy　（D）the navy would start

文法の小箱

構造の理解

　第 12 パラグラフの文、The main guns could lob a 1½-ton shell 42 km, meaning a round fired from Tokyo Tower in Minato Ward could reach Kamakura Station in Kanagawa Prefecture. を解説します。

　42 km は副詞的に lob を修飾し、lob ... 42 km が意味するものとして、meaning 以下で説明しています。meaning ... は which means ... という非制限関係節で置き換えることができます。fired from ... Minato Ward の句は a round を修飾し、a round は、meaning が導く節内の主語で、could reach ... が動詞句となっています。

　could は仮定法を示しており、この文の試訳は「主砲は 1.5 トンの砲弾を 42km 飛ばすことができた。これは、港区の東京タワーから発射された砲弾が神奈川県の鎌倉駅まで届く距離である（実際にそういうことはないが…）。」となります。

Interpretation and Composition 🖊 日➡英

以下の日本語をよく読んで、下線部のみを通訳してください。

1. ペリー来航のあと四国の宇和島藩は黒船建造にのりだした。苦労の連続であった。たとえば蒸気機関が馬力不足であり、さらにはボイラーも破裂したようだ。技術的には「蒸気エネルギーをピストンの上下運動に変換し」、次に「上下運動を回転運動に変換すれば外輪が動く」ことは知られていた。黒船係の者たちは歯車と回転軸を絶妙に組み合わせてようやくこの問題を克服できたという。蘭学者の協力と無名の職人たちの成し遂げたことである。

　　ヒント 上下運動 vertical motion ／回転運動 rotary motion ／回転軸 axle of wheels ／外輪 paddle wheel ／歯車 cogwheels

2. 日本も江戸期の初め頃までは海外にけっこう出かけていた。多帆の朱印船は天測航法器材を使用して大洋を航海する術も持っていたが、徳川幕府は海外渡航を禁じた。ついで船舶の技術も凍結させた。むろん海洋船の建造は固く禁じた。「海を制するもの」は政権を覆す力を持つからだ。

> ヒント 多帆の with masts and sails ／天測航法器材 measuring device for celestial navigation ／朱印 Japanese merchant ships bound overseas with official permit, red seal ships ／海洋船 ocean-going ship ／海を制する dominant in sea power

---

深掘りの視点

海上戦略勢力としてのヴァイキング船団

　島国にとって敵性海上勢力は恐ろしいものでした。今では潜在的脅威に航空戦力が加わって（海上、海中、空中と3次元的に）より複雑化しています。古くはヴァイキング船団が海上戦略勢力としての足跡を歴史に残しています。

　ヴァイキングの正確な定義は難しいですが、ここでは「北方の民」でスカンジナビア半島やデンマークにいた人たちであるとしておきます。特に8世紀から12世紀ごろまで活動していました。独特のヴァイキング船に乗り込み、ヨーロッパ諸国に侵攻して略奪を繰返していました。

　農地や牧畜地を荒らすことが多くあったので、諸国から非常に恐れられました。イングランド（ブリテン島）にも出現してその大半を征服しました。

　冒険心に富むヴァイキングは遠くまで遠征して方々に出現しました。南イタリア、パリ、シシリー島も攻撃の対象になりました。彼らの出現とともにノルマン（Norman）諸国が方々にできました。そのうち被征服民とも混血して同化したものが多く、また、途中でキリスト教を受け入れてキリスト教徒になった人たちも多くいました。英語に北欧系統の単語が多いのもヴァイキングの影響が大きいと言えます。

　8世紀から11世紀にかけては、イングランド北部および東部に対して繰り返し彼らの攻撃と侵入が行われました。イングランドの文化の中心は、そのせいもあり南部の Wessex 地方に移りました。そこは King Alfred（849-899）の統治する国であり、ヴァイキングの侵攻をかろうじて防いでいました。この王は教育の推進と文化の維持とに力を注いだことでも知られています。

　アングロ・サクソン年代記（Anglo-Saxon Chronicle）もこの王の影響のもとに成立しました。しかし、英国北部（Northumberland）や中部地方（Mercian）で書かれた多くの文学や記録はヴァイキングの侵攻により消滅しています。

　幸いにいくつかの作品は West-Saxon 方言で書き換えられて今日に伝わっています。その代表が叙事詩 Beowulf であり、古代スウェーデン王の活躍を描いています。当時のスカンジナビアの生活の様子を知るには大変貴重な書物です。

UNIT 6

社会

Schools and students look to boost youth voter turnout

若い人たちの投票率を上げる試み

With just days to go before the Upper House election, schools and students in Japan are working to encourage young people to cast their ballots.

① They hope to boost voter turnout among young people, which (あ) [　　　　] low since the minimum voting age was lowered from 20 to 18 in 2016.

② The July 10 election for the House of Councilors, the upper chamber of parliament, will be the fifth national election since the age limit was lowered.

③ (イ) At Tokyo Metropolitan Nogyo High School in the city of Fuchu, senior students were given an opportunity to cast ballots in a mock election held as part of a class last Tuesday.

④ Using election bulletins and "vote match" services that help people find political parties and candidates whose policies best align with their views, participants compared the actual candidates running for Upper House seats from Tokyo. They then wrote the names of (い) [candidates of choice] on the ballot.

⑤ The mock election "helped me learn about the importance of elections," said Remi Shimada, 18. "I want to exercise the voting right given to me."

⑥ At Ritsumeikan University in Kyoto Prefecture, a booth was set up on June 22 to help students who live away from their registered residences but who hope to cast absentee ballots.

⑦ (ロ) The action, led by Ryotaro Matsuo, a law major, and Haruki Masui, a College of Social Sciences student, came after a similar booth was established for the first time on the campus for last October's Lower House election.

⑧ The first booth was created after Masui, who hails from Osaka Prefecture, had difficulty completing the procedures necessary for casting an absentee ballot.

⑨ "We hope to make (う) [　　　] known that voters can cast absentee ballots even though their residence is not registered where they live," Matsuo said. "We want more people to vote."

⑩ The booth for the Upper House election distributes copies of a manual that explains how to apply for absentee ballots, while staff can answer questions from other students. (ハ) On Wednesday, they held an event that saw a law professor specializing in electoral systems offer explanations.

⑪ At Iwate Prefectural University, a group of students are also helping others planning to cast absentee ballots.

⑫ Atsushi Endo, a senior student $_{(え)}$ [at / of] the university's Faculty of Policy Studies, studied the absentee voting system at a seminar and realized that the system remains unknown to many students.

⑬ Endo and friends who attended the seminar opened a booth to help other students with procedures for absentee ballots for last year's Lower House election.

⑭ For the July 10 election, they formed a larger group to provide assistance, while also holding a tour that took participants to the offices of candidates in the Iwate constituency.

⑮ "To students, politics and elections are in a different world," Endo said. "We hope our tour and other activities will allow many to find $_{(お)}$ those things familiar."

(July 3, 2022 | The Japan Times delivered by JIJI)

---

the Upper House 上院［日本では参議院（the House of Councilors)］/ turnout 投票者数 / Tokyo Metropolitan Nogyo High School 東京都立農業高校 / vote match ボートマッチ（選挙に関するインターネットサービス）/ Iwate Prefectural University 岩手県立大学 / Faculty of Political Studies（岩手県立大学）総合政策学部 / constituency 選挙区

Vocabulary Check

定義欄から適切なものを選んで単語の意味・内容を確認しておきましょう。

［単語］

1．boost　　2．mock　　3．align with　　4．run for　　　　5．exercise

6．absentee　7．major　8．hail from　　9．specialize in　10．participant

［定義欄］

a. to use some power; put something into action

b. to be from; to come from

c. to stand as a candidate; to come forward as a candidate

d. to deal with some specific field of science; to concentrate on a special branch of study

e. to increase in number

f. a student of some specific field of science

g. to side with; to agree to some extent with; to go along fairly with

h. a person unable to be at the polls at election time

i. one who takes part in some event; one who takes a share with others in some activity

j. sham; pretended in the way something seems to be actually conducted

---

深堀りの視点

期日前投票と不在者投票の違い

　期日前投票とは、選挙当日よりも前の日に、選挙人名簿に登録された住所地で直接投票箱に投票する方法です。選挙当日、仕事・旅行・冠婚葬祭・その他の行事などで投票できない人が行う投票の方法です。

　一方、不在者投票とは、仕事や旅行の関係で期日前投票すらできない人が、滞在先の選挙管理委員会で投票用紙を投票日前に提出する方法です。

　なお、在外選挙制度というのがあり、これは、仕事や留学などで海外に住んでいる人向けの投票制度で、滞在している国の在外公館や郵送などで投票することができます。

　ちなみに、選挙の公示と告示は異なります。衆議院総選挙と参議院通常選挙は「公示」され、衆議院・参議院の補欠選挙、都道府県の知事および議員選挙、市町村の長および議員選挙は「告示」されます。どちらも選挙が行われることを知らせることですが、「公示」は憲法7条に基づき、天皇の国事行為に伴います。

Stream of the Article

　この英文全体を読むと以下のような構成になります。記号（a）から（e）までの内容を記述して、この構成分析を完成させてください。

1．学校は投票者数を増やしたいと考えている。というのは 2016 年に投票できる年齢が 20 歳から 18 歳に引き下げられて以来、ずっと低い水準だから。
2．今回の選挙は、投票年齢引き下げ後、（a　　　　　）回目の国政選挙である。
3．東京都立農業高校では、模擬選挙を（b　　　　　）の一環として行った。
4．立命館大学では、（c　　　　　）投票を希望する学生のために、ブースが設定された。
5．岩手県立大学では、（d　　　　　）年生の遠藤君が選挙当日に選挙に行けない人が投票するシステムを学んだが、多くの学生がそのシステムを知らないことがわかった。
6．7 月 10 日に向けて、選挙の手助けをするためにグループを作り、岩手（e　　　　　）の候補者の事務所に訪問するというツアーも企画した。

Interpretation and Translation 🖉 英➡日

1．③パラグラフの下線部（イ）の意味を日本語で表してください。

2．⑦パラグラフの下線部（ロ）の意味を日本語で表してください。

_____

_____

3．⑩パラグラフの下線部（ハ）の意味を日本語で表してください。

_____

_____

attend の語法

　第 13 パラグラフ 1 行目に attended the seminar とあります。この句における attend は、「〜に出席する」ですが、「に」を at や to と思って、attend at 〜や attend to 〜のような表現は、この意味にはなりません。

　attend at 〜の表現はありませんが、attend to 〜は「〜に専念する、〜に注意して聞く、（客や注文などに）応じる」の意味となります。

　　He should attend to his work.
　　彼は自分の仕事に専念すべきだ。
　　Attend to what she is saying.
　　彼女が言っていることに耳を傾けなさい。
　　Are you being attended to?
　　ご用を承っておりますか？（店員が客に話しかける言葉）
　硬い表現ですが、他動詞用法で「〜に伴う」という意味があります。
　　Great danger may attend the experiment.
　　非常な危険がその実験に伴うかもしれない。

Grammar and Comprehension

1．（あ）の ［　　］ に入れるのに文法的・文脈的に最も適切な形を下から選んでください。
　（A）has left　（B）have left　（C）has remained　（D）have remained

2．（い）の ［　　］ 内を適切な名詞句にするにはどうすればよいか、下から選んでください。
　（A）the candidates of the choice　（B）the candidates of their choice
　（C）their candidates of the choice　（D）their candidates of their choice

3．（う）の［　　］に入れるのに文法的・文脈的に最も適切な形を下から選んでください。
（A）it　（B）there　（C）you　（D）one

4．（え）の［　　］の中の前置詞のうち正しいほうを選んでください。
［　　　　　　　］

5．（お）の下線部 those が表すものとして最も適切なものを下から選んでください。
（A）students　　　　　　　　　（B）politics and elections
（C）our tour and other activities　（D）many

Interpretation and Composition ✏日➡英

次の日本語を英語に訳してください。

1．日蓮は、佐渡に流罪になったとき、快適な暮らしをするのは困難であったが、そこで仏教的考えに関するいくつかの本を書いた。

　ヒント ～に流罪となる be exiled to ～／～するのは困難である have difficulty doing ～

_____

_____

_____

2．日本人は、神仏習合にもとづく宗教的寛容性があるので、ほとんどの日本人が神社もお寺も両方ともお詣りする。

　ヒント 神仏習合 the syncretization of Shinto with Buddhism ／ X があるので、Y は～する（ことができる）
　　　　X allows Y to do ～

_____

_____

_____

文法の小箱 分詞の形容詞用法：given to me と given me のどっちが自然？

　第5パラグラフに the voting right given to me とありますが、これが the voting right given me とならない理由があります。

　これは、The voting right is given to me.（以下の③文）という文を名詞化した形です。受動態への変形前の文（能動態）は、省略されている主語を、例えば、the government として、以下の①文（第3文型）を想定できます。この①文は、以下の②文（第4文型）に書き換えても意味は大きく変わりません。

　　① The government gives the voting right to me.

　　② The government gives me the voting right.

　　③ The voting right is given to me.

　　④ The voting right is given me.

　①文を基本文と捉えると、①→③の変形より、①→②→④への変形のほうが複雑になります。変形のプロセスが複雑なほど、非文法性が高まる（不自然になる）という考え方があります。

　なお、①文と②文は、意味内容は変わりませんが、ニュアンス（強調点）が異なります。①文は to me を強調する文であるのに対し、②文は the voting right を強調する文です。この違いがわかる訳を挙げておきます。

　　①政府が投票権を与えるのは私に対してである。

　　②政府が私に与えるのは投票権である。

　英文の①と②が答えとなる疑問文は、それぞれ、（1）（2）となります。

　　（1）To whom does the government give the voting right?

　　（2）What does the government give to me?

社会

Restitution, but at what price?
お金に換算できるのか？

As Holocaust cases mount, some worry that history's greatest horror is being cheapened

◁| 07

① Bernard Lieberman was reared a child of privilege in a small town outside Lodz, Poland. He was one of nine children in an Orthodox Jewish family that lived largely off the money of affluent relatives and regularly opened up its home to poor neighbors. But that comfortable life swiftly ended on Sept. 1, 1939, when the Nazis stormed into Poland. Only 19, Bernard was soon separated from his siblings and transported from camp to camp, (あ) [   ] time in Auschwitz-Birkenau.

② Bernard (who later changed his last name from Lieberman to Lee) made it out of the war alive, but he lost his entire family. Now, like many survivors, he is fighting to get something back. In October he joined a class action filed in the Federal District Court of New York against Dresdner Bank, where a wealthy family member had an account. "There were 6 million people who were murdered, and every family had something," says Lee. "Our things do not belong to them, and justice will be done when (い) they are given back."

③ Demands for justice from Holocaust survivors like Lee are steadily mounting. In August, Switzerland's two largest banks agreed to pay $1.25 billion to settle wartime claims against them. (イ) Since then, no fewer than 10 class actions have been filed against European companies that do business in the U.S. Some of these are claims for individual accounts confiscated by banks in Germany and Austria. Others charge that major corporations such as Krupp, Volkswagen and Daimler-Benz profited from slave labor during the wartime years and should pay billions in back wages and other compensation. The issue of Holocaust reparations was raised again at a conference in Washington last week sponsored by the State Department and the U.S. Holocaust Memorial Museum, where representatives from 44 countries discussed the restitution of artworks and other Holocaust-era assets.

④ Amid all this, (う) [   ], a small but growing segment of the survivor community is questioning whether the campaign for restitution has gone too far and is sending the wrong message. "This is not how the survivors want the Holocaust to be remembered," says Roman Kent, chairman of the American Gathering of Jewish Holocaust Survivors. "The image and memory of those killed have been put in the background, and all I hear about now is the glitter of gold." Abraham Foxman, the national director of the Anti-Defamation League, voices a similar concern: "Survivors who have claims deserve to bring them forward, but it's at a heavy price. The next generation will believe it's all about money."

⑤ Or all about lawyers. With so many suits, competing attorneys have taken to squabbling publicly over how to proceed and how to divvy up the spoils. In recent months attorneys (え) [crisscross] the U.S. and Europe to pack their rosters with survivors; in some cases, they have rushed to file competing claims against the same company in different states. The lawyers involved in these cases argue that the civil justice system is the only mode of recourse. "You can't send a company to jail for these things," says Washington attorney Michael Hausfeld, who helped slap Ford with a slave-labor suit last March. (ロ) Both Ford and General Motors have been fighting charges, reported last week in the Washington Post, that their German subsidiaries aided the Nazi war effort. Ford has admitted that its German plants were seized by the Nazis, but the company maintains that it severed all ties to these outposts during the war. GM issued a statement "categorically denying" that it aided the Nazis in World War II.

⑥ Others contend that even if the charges are true, the pursuit of monetary restitution is misdirected. "When you're taking money from Volkswagen today, it's coming not from the Nazis but from a 30-year-old German," says Harvard University law professor Alan Dershowitz. (ハ) Then there's the question of who is entitled to the money from any settlements. Survivors have yet to see a dime from the Swiss settlement, because lawyers and Jewish organizations are still hammering out the details. Under one proposal being floated by the World Jewish Restitution Organization, after specific claims are settled, 80% of what's left would go to destitute survivors and 20% to Holocaust education. Gizella Wiesshaus, the 69-year-old survivor who brought the first claim against the Swiss banks, protested this kind of arrangement outside the State Department conference last week, claiming that the money should go only to (お) [   ] who suffered.

⑦ Many claimants, like Bernard Lee, have pledged to give anything they receive to charity. Yet time is not on their side. Lee, who is 77 and was recently hospitalized for heart trouble, is worried that "every day some new survivor passes away." The lawyers, undoubtedly, will carry on.

(December 14, 1998 | TIME)

---

restitution 損害賠償 / privilege 特別（扱い）、特権 / siblings 兄弟姉妹 / Auschwitz-Birkenau アウシュビッツ＝ビルケナウ強制収容所 / class action 集団訴訟 / account 口座 / claim 賠償請求 / repatriation 資産等の回復（復帰）/ asset 資産 / segment 一部分（ある人たち）/ defamation 名誉棄損 / attorney 法定代理人（弁護士）/ take to squabbling = to begin quarreling 激しい口論になる / spoils 略奪品 / crisscross 縦横に走る、あちこち行く / roster 名簿 / mode やり方（手段）/ recourse 頼みの綱 / subsidiary 子会社 / sever = to cut ～ off 切り離す / outpost 前哨隊、前哨地 / carry on（仕事を）続ける

Vocabulary Check

定義欄から適切なものを選んで単語の意味・内容を確認しておきましょう。

[単語]

　　1．live off ～　　　2．do time　　　3．file　　　4．settle　5．confiscate

　　6．bring forward　7．divvy up ～　8．slap A with B　9．contend　10．entitle

[定義欄]

　a. to take and keep　　　　　　　　b. to present

　c. to hit or punish ～ with ～　　　d. to depend on ～ for one's existence

　e. to give a right to ～　　　　　　f. to come to agreement about ～

　g. to offer for consideration　　　　h. to divide and share

　i. to undergo a period of imprisonment　j. to declare

深掘りの視点

Saint と Apocalypse の定義など

　The Oxford Modern English Dictionary では A saint is a holy or canonized person regarded as having a place in heaven と定義します。「天国にいる」聖なる人とされています。canonize は「聖人として認める」という意味です。名詞形は canonization であり、紛らわしいのが① canon と② cannon です。

　①は canon または Canon と表記して「戒律」「聖人の一覧表や名簿」「ミサの典文」「正典」などの意味。apocrypha は「外典」の意味。

　② a cannon は「台座付きの大砲」「機関砲」などの意味。さらに a cannon ball は「砲弾」やテニスでの「弾丸サーブ」の意味。

　Apocalypse は「ヨハネの黙示録」「終末」の意味です。小文字で表記すれば「大惨事」「大破壊」「惨劇」などの意味。「黙示録」の場合は Revelation to John と表記する場合もあります。

Stream of the Article

　この英文全体を読むと以下のような構成になります。記号（a）から（e）までの内容を記述して、この構成分析を完成させてください。

1．Bernard Lieberman さんが青年期に体験した収容所生活
2．Bernard さんは集団訴訟に加わった。
　　「奪われた財産等」の（a　　　　）を求めている。
3．同様の集団訴訟は増えている。
　　具体例（1）（b　　　　）の二大銀行の件
　　具体例（2）ヨーロッパ系の会社の件
4．そのような訴訟に対して疑問の声もある。
　　具体例（c　　　　）だけの問題なのか？
5．（d　　　　）の問題でもある。
　　具体例　弁護士が同一の被告訴企業を相手に競争状態
6．訴訟で勝ち得た返還金は誰のものか？
7．原告には（e　　　　）との闘いになってきている。

Interpretation and Translation 英➡日

1．③パラグラフの下線部（イ）の意味を日本語で表してください。

_____

_____

2．⑤パラグラフの下線部（ロ）の意味を日本語で表してください。

_____

_____

3．⑥パラグラフの下線部（ハ）の意味を日本語で表してください。

_____

_____

表現の泉

Assumption, Saint, Blessed の意味

　名詞の綴りを大文字で始める英語には「個人名」「地名」「宗教関連」などが考えられます。キリスト教関連では Christmas（クリスマス）、the Holy Scripture（聖書）、the Holy See（ローマ教皇庁、聖座 [＝ the papacy]）、Holy Communion [＝ the celebration of the Eucharist]（聖体拝領 [のパンと葡萄酒]）、Holy Thursday（聖木曜日 [＝復活祭前の木曜日]）などですが、少しなじみがないのが the Assumption（聖母被昇天 [の祝日]）でしょう。

　Assumption は紀元 13 世紀ごろから英語でも使用され始めました。この祝日は 8 月 15 日で、日本ではお盆と終戦記念の日に相当します。意味は the taking up of a person into heaven、つまり「聖母マリアが神の国にあげられた」という意味ですが、主にカトリック教会の用語です。

　「聖人」は比較的よく知られていて、Saint ～ と書けば「聖～」と意味になります。Saint Mark「聖マルコ」、Saint John「聖ヨハネ」となります。St. John と表記することもあります。

　Blessed（福者）もまたカトリックの称号です。blessed の定義は次の通りです。Blessed is a title given to a dead person as an acknowledgement of his or her holy life; beatify. beatify は「福者として認める」の意味もあります。

Grammar and Comprehension

1．（あ）の ［　　］に入れるのに最も適切な形を下から選んでください。
　（A）do　（B）did　（C）done　（D）doing

2．（い）の下線部 they の指している内容を下から選んでください。
　（A）many survivors　（B）6 million people
　（C）our things　　　（D）Bank accounts

3．（う）の ［　　］に入れるのに最も適切な単語を下から選んでください。
　（A）but　（B）however　（C）although　（D）notwithstanding

4．（え）の ［　　］内の単語をどのように変えたら文法的であるか適切な形を下から選んでください。
　（A）crisscross　（B）crisscrosses　（C）have crisscrossed　（D）to crisscross

5．（お）の ［　　］内に入れるのに最も適切な単語を下から選んでください。
　（A）ones　（B）these　（C）those　（D）them

文法の小箱

自動詞と他動詞の違い

第4パラグラフに hear about ～（～について［詳しく］聞いている）が出てきました（p.48，1行目）が、ほかの自動詞表現に hear of ～（～の噂を聞く）があります。

about には「詳しく」、of には「ちょっと」のニュアンスがあります。たとえば、talk of ～（～の噂をする）と talk about ～（～について［いろいろ］語る）の違いがあります。

一方、他動詞の場合は、「直接」の意味があります。

例1：I heard her play the piano.（私は彼女がピアノを弾くのを聞いた）

例2：He talked his father into buying a car.（彼は父親を説得して車を買ってもらった）

※例1は彼女がピアノを弾くのを直接聞いたことを表し、例2は父親に直接話しかけたことを意味する（父親のことを話しているのではない）。

Interpretation and Composition 🖊 日➡英

以下の日本語をよく読んで、下線部のみを通訳してください。

1. 時代が過ぎればわからなくなることはあるものだ。たとえば、天保11年（1840）生まれの渋沢栄一だが、若い時に攘夷を決行しようと思っていた。はるか後年、70歳の頃には「やはり攘夷の気分でもよかったのではないか」という趣旨の発言をしている。翁が憤懣やるかたなしと感じたのは、米国カリフォルニア州の日本人学童への差別的隔離待遇（1906-1907）と排日移民運動（1912）に対するものであった。

   ヒント 攘夷 expel foreigners ／～という趣旨の to the effect that ～

   _____

   _____

   _____

2. 1906年のこと、サンフランシスコ市の大地震に際して日本政府は国家予算（概算5億円）のおよそ0.1%の金額を見舞金として拠出している。これは現代の国家予算で換算すれば1,000億円ほどであろう。その見返りが日本人学童らに対する差別待遇か！と当時の日本人は憤慨し、渋沢翁もこれには落胆した。

   ヒント 国家予算 national budget ／見舞金 money gift as a token of sympathy and condolence ／換算する convert into ～, change into ～

   _____

   _____

   _____

社会

8 The New Testament's unsolved mysteries
新約聖書の謎

⦿ 08

①   Archaeology may have cast doubt on the historicity of such Old Testament characters as Moses and Abraham, but what of the central figure of the New? Was Jesus of Nazareth a real person who trod the dusty roads of Palestine in the 1ˢᵗ century? Or were his life, death and resurrection, as recorded in the four Gospels, events that belong entirely to the realm of faith?

②   Science has neither proved nor disproved the existence of the itinerant preacher and wonder worker ₍ぁ₎ [believe / Christians / was / who] the Son of God. ₍ィ₎ <u>After all, writes biblical scholar R.T. France, "no 1ˢᵗ century inscription mentions him and no object or building has survived which has a specific link to him."</u> Nonetheless, recent finds in the Holy Land have provided a wealth of insights into the milieu from which belief in Christ emerged.

③   The most controversial of these discoveries were the 800 or so Hebrew and Aramaic texts unearthed during the 1940s from caves near the Dead Sea. Biblicists have long hoped to locate more of them; last month Israeli archaeologists began excavating four newly discovered caves in the same area.

④   ₍ロ₎ <u>Scholars originally thought that the Dead Sea Scrolls, with their tantalizing references to the imminent coming of a Messiah, represented the quirky tenets of a fringe sect of Jewish ascetics known as Essenes.</u> But experts now believe that the texts, which include fragments of legal codes, oracles and other literary genres, ₍い₎ [   ] in 1ˢᵗ century Judaism.

⑤   The Holy Land of Jesus' time, the scrolls show, was rife with apocalyptic fervor. Ordinary Jews yearned for a savior who would lead them in a holy war against the oppressive Romans and a corrupt aristocracy, typified by the hated King Herod. Some scholars believe that Jesus was one of many political rebels in Palestine. His proclamation that the meek would inherit the earth was, in this view, not a dream of eschatological hope but a here-and-now demand for a new political order.

⑥   Recent manuscript and inscription finds indicate that such biblical names as Joseph and Judas were commonly used in the 1ˢᵗ century. One of those discoveries is especially intriguing. In 1990, diggers in the Jewish Quarter of Jerusalem's Old City uncovered an

53

ossuary (repository for bones) with the inscription Joseph Son of Caiaphas. This marked the first archaeological evidence that the high priest Caiaphas, who according to the Gospels presided at the Sanhedrin's trial of Jesus, was a real person. So, indisputably, was Pilate. In 1961, diggers in Caesarea found the fragment of a plaque indicating that a building had been dedicated by PONTUS PILATUS, PREFECT OF JUDEA.

⑦ Nazareth, which many scholars contend was the most probable site of Jesus' birth (rather than Bethlehem), was a small agricultural village in the 1ˢᵗ century. It is only about an hour's walk from Sepphoris, a major commercial center where, according to recent excavations, Romans, Jews, and (later) Christians once lived and worked in considerable harmony. ₍ᵤₐ₎ <u>Sepphoris is not mentioned in the New Testament, but some scholars speculate that Jesus, a carpenter by trade, might have found work there. If so, he may have been exposed to a wider range of cultures and ideas than his origins in rustic Nazareth would suggest.</u> Did he, for example, learn to speak Greek, the common language of Rome's empire, as well as Aramaic and Hebrew?

⑧ ₍ᵤ₎ [   ] community that played a major role in Jesus' life is Capernaum on the Sea of Galilee. ₍ₑ₎ It was there, according to the Gospels, that he began his public ministry, probably in A.D. 28. Archaeologists have uncovered a 1ˢᵗ century house in Capernaum that according to tradition was the home of St. Peter. The building contains a meeting room that might have been used for worship. Some experts speculate that this was the synagogue where Jesus preached, as recounted in *John* 6:59.

⑨ The Gospels contain no fewer than 45 references to boats and fishing as they relate to Jesus. In 1986, two members of a Galilean kibbutz came across the remains of ₍ₒ₎ [   ] 8-m-long wooden dory, buried in the mud near Kinneret on the Sea of Galilee, that has been carbon-dated to the 1ˢᵗ century. Almost certainly, this was the kind of vessel used by Peter, James, John and the other fisherfolk whom Jesus recruited as his first disciples.

⑩ Time and again, archaeological finds have validated scriptural references. Discoveries of an astonishing variety of 1ˢᵗ century coins, for example, help explain the need for money changers, whom an angry Jesus drove away from Jerusalem's Great Temple. Still, there are many questions that archaeology cannot now answer. Did Pilate pass judgement on Jesus at the Antonia fortress near the Temple site, or at Herod's palace across town? (If the latter, then, the famed Via Dolorosa — the route that Jesus followed carrying his cross to Golgotha — is incorrect.) Is the tomb of Jesus beneath the Church of the Holy Sepulcher, as tradition holds, or some place unknown outside the Old City's walls?

⑪ Science may never say. Many devout believers do not care. For them, the divinely inspired testimony of the Gospels is infinitely more reliable than any evidence unearthed by the hammers of archaeology.

(December 18, 1995 | TIME)

inscription 碑文、碑銘 / milieu 状況、環境 / tenet 教義 / ascetic 苦行者 / oracle 神の言葉、神託 / fervor 熱情 / the meek 従順な人々 / ossuary 骨壺 / plaque 銘板 / ministry 布教活動 / dory（底が平らな）小型 の船 / validate = to confirm / devout 信心深い / testimony 証言

☆背景知識の注釈

Nazareth ナザレ（地名）/ Holy Land 聖地（エルサレム）/ Aramaic アラム語（古代シリア地方の言葉）/ Dead Sea Scrolls 死海文書 / Messiah 救い主 / Essenes エッセネ派信徒（BC2 ～ AD1 にパレスチナに存在したユダヤ教の一派）/ King Herod ヘロデ王（ユダヤの王）/ Jewish Quarter of Jerusalem's Old City エルサレム旧市街地のユダヤ人居住区 / Bethlehem ベツレヘム（地名）/ Caiaphas カヤパ（人名）［イエスの裁判を主催した大祭司］/ Sanhedrin 古代エルサレムの最高法院 / Caesarea カエサリア（地名）［イスラエル北西部の古代の港町］/ PONTUS PILATUS ポンティオ・ピラト（人名）/ PREFECT OF JUDEA ユダヤ総督（知事）/ Sepphoris セフォリス（地名）［古代ガリラヤ地方の一部］/ Gospels 福音書 / Capernaum カペルナウム（地名）［ガリラヤ湖に面する古都］/ John 6:59 ヨハネの福音 6 章 59 節 / Kibbutz キブツ（イスラエルの集団農場）/ Kinneret キネレト［ガリラヤ湖（= the Sea of Galilee）の南西沿岸の町］/ Antonia fortress アントニア要塞（エルサレム神殿に隣接して存在した要塞）/ Via Dolorosa 十字架の道行き（苦難の道）/ Golgotha ゴルゴタ（イエス・キリストが十字架刑を受けたとされる場所）/ Holy Sepulcher 聖墳墓（キリストの墓）

Vocabulary Check

定義欄から適切なものを選んで単語の意味・内容を確認しておきましょう。

[単語]

1．tread　　2．itinerant　　3．tantalize　　4．quirky　　5．rife with
6．apocalyptic　7．eschatological　8．intriguing　9．rustic　10．recount

[定義欄]

a. relating to the destruction of the world

b. to walk on ～

c. relating to the theory concerned with death, judgement, and destiny

d. rural

e. full of ～

f. to torment or tease by showing what one wants but that one cannot obtains

g. having unexpected habits or ideas

h. traveling from place to place

i. to tell or to give an account of ～

j. arousing curiosity

Stream of the Article

　この英文全体を読むと以下のような構成になります。記号（a）から（e）までの内容を記述して、この構成分析を完成させてください。

1．考古学が疑問を投げかける歴史的人物
　　具体例（1）：旧約のモーゼ、アブラハム
　　具体例（2）：ナザレのイエス
2．死海文書のもたらした見解
　　具体例：（a　　　　　）はもうすぐ来る→この見解は広く受け入れられていたユダヤ人の考えを反映している。
3．（b　　　　　）熱気が漂うイエス時代の聖地
4．最近の古文書や碑文の発見したこと
　　具体例（1）：高位聖職者（c　　　　　）は実在の人物
　　具体例（2）：ユダヤ総督ピラトも実在の人物
5．新たな可能性
　　具体例（1）：イエス生誕の地はナザレ？
　　具体例（2）：商業都市セフォリスでイエスは異文化の影響を受けた？
6．ガリラヤ湖畔カペルナウムでの発見
　　具体例（1）：ヨハネ6章59節にあるように（d　　　　　）が説教をしたシナゴーグか？
　　具体例（2）：使徒たちの使用したのと同型の小舟の発見
7．考古学の発見は聖書の記述を裏付けるものが多い。
8．謎は残る。
　　具体例（1）：ピラトのイエスに対する判決はどこで行われたのか？
　　具体例（2）：（e　　　　　）の地下にあるのがイエスの墓なのか？
9．考古学的発見は熱心な信者の信仰とは関係がないようだ。

Interpretation and Translation 　英➡日

1．②パラグラフの下線部（イ）の意味を日本語で表してください。

＿＿＿＿＿＿＿＿＿＿＿＿＿＿＿＿＿＿＿＿＿＿＿＿＿＿＿＿＿＿＿＿＿＿

＿＿＿＿＿＿＿＿＿＿＿＿＿＿＿＿＿＿＿＿＿＿＿＿＿＿＿＿＿＿＿＿＿＿

2．④パラグラフの下線部（ロ）の意味を日本語で表してください。

＿＿＿＿＿＿＿＿＿＿＿＿＿＿＿＿＿＿＿＿＿＿＿＿＿＿＿＿＿＿＿＿＿＿

＿＿＿＿＿＿＿＿＿＿＿＿＿＿＿＿＿＿＿＿＿＿＿＿＿＿＿＿＿＿＿＿＿＿

3．⑦パラグラフの下線部（ハ）の意味を日本語で表してください。

_____

_____

表現の泉

recount と re-count

第8パラグラフ最後に recount（詳しく話す）がありますが、re の直後にハイフンを入れたら別の意味の単語になります。re は「再」の意味を持つ接頭辞なので、re-count は「再度計算する→数え直す」の意味となります。

同様に、次のような組もあります。

例1：recover（回復する）、re-cover（再度被せる）

例2：reform（改善する）、re-form（作り直す）

Grammar and Comprehension

1．（あ）の［　　］内の単語を正しく並べ替えてください。

「　　　　　　　　　　　　　　　　　」

2．（い）の［　　］内に入れるべき正しい文法的表現を選んでください。

　（A）widely reflect held beliefs

　（B）reflect held widely beliefs

　（C）widely held beliefs reflect

　（D）reflect beliefs widely held

3．（う）の［　　］に入るべき語句を選んでください。

　（A）Other　（B）Another　（C）The other　（D）The others

4．（え）の下線部の It と同じ用法の it が入っている文を選んでください。

　（A）I bought a book last week. Now I find it more intriguing than when I bought it.

　（B）It rained cats and dogs yesterday, which made me unable to participate in the event.

　（C）To pass the exam, I think it unnecessary to review all the things I learned in the class.

　（D）Is it a bell that according to Shinto will drive away evil spirits when rung at a shrine?

5．（お）の［　　］に次のどの冠詞を入れると文法的・文脈的に適切ですか。

　（A）a　（B）an　（C）the

構造の理解

　第3パラグラフ第1文、The most controversial of these discoveries were the 800 or so Hebrew and Aramaic texts unearthed during the 1940s from caves near the Dead Sea. を解説します。

　the 800 以下が主語で、the most controversial ... discoveries が補語の倒置構文です（CVS となっています）。また、unearthed 以下が the 800 ... texts を修飾しています。

　この部分の試訳は「これらの発見に関して最も議論の余地があるのが、1940 年代に死海近くの洞穴から発掘された 800 ぐらいのヘブライ語とアラム語の文献でした。」となります。

Interpretation and Composition 🖊 日 ➡ 英

以下の日本語をよく読んで、下線部のみを通訳してください。

1．漢文には「将（はた）春秋」という表現がある。春秋（史書）のように記録しているのか？という意味だ。<u>この書はその修辞に満ちた筆法のみならず君主や国王に対しても遠慮しない記述で有名である。ところで新約聖書もイエスに対してかなり遠慮せずに書いているようだ。</u>

　ヒント　この書（春秋）The annals　＊「春秋」The Spring and Autumn Annals of Zhou states

_____

_____

_____

2．たとえばマルコ3章21節には「その親族のものイエスを取り押さへんと出できたる」「彼を狂せりと謂ひてなり」とある。これはしかし「宗教的高揚感を心配して」のことだとギリシャ語では読めるそうだ。<u>身内がはらはらするほどに説教に熱弁をふるい、熱情のあまり卓を拳で叩かれたのだろうか？</u>

　ヒント　高揚感 exhilaration, with lively cheerfulness ／熱情 relentless excitement, passion

_____

_____

_____

深掘りの視点

死海文書と謎

1947 年に死海の北岸で発見された死海文書（Dead Sea Scroll）はユダヤ教エッセネ派の実態を相当程度に解き明かしたとされています。そしてキリスト教の起源をここに求める考えの人たちもいるようです。

また、新約聖書には洗礼者ヨハネが登場します。英語でも John the Baptist と表現するように洗礼の儀式を行った人物ですが、誰を相手に行ったのでしょうか？　またヨハネはユダヤ教エッセネ派の人物なのでしょうか？

ヨハネは（1）誰にでも洗礼を受けるように呼び掛けています、（2）洗礼の準備期間はありません、（3）洗礼の回数は一度だけです。これに対してエッセネ派（クムラン教団）では何度も繰り返し行う清めの儀式であったとされます。つまりヨハネとエッセネ派は完全に同じではありません。

クムラン教団跡の発掘により洗礼のための浴槽が発見されているので、洗礼を重要視していたことは確かでしょう。さらにはパリサイ派にも洗礼を重んじる人たちが存在したとされ、彼らは「洗礼パリサイ派」とでもいう存在でした。イエスと対立したパリサイ派ですが、洗礼の儀式を持つという点でもキリスト教と共通することころがあります。

イエス自身も子供時代はユダヤ教徒として生活していますが、その実態はよくわかりません。そしてイエスと洗礼者ヨハネの関係や、ヨハネとエッセネ派の教団との関係などは完全に解明されたわけではありません。まだ多くの謎は残っているのです！

経済

9 Campaigning parties must present specific measures to boost power supply
エネルギー問題を考える

① Many people are increasingly concerned about how long the power crunch will continue amid the scorching heat. In their debates for the House of Councillors election, political parties are urged to present concrete measures to ensure a stable supply of electricity.

② In late June, the government issued a power crunch advisory for the first time in the service area of Tokyo Electric Power Company Holdings, Inc. This step was taken as electricity demand was expected to surge due to unseasonably hot weather. Although the government got through the situation by requesting households and (あ) [   ] to conserve electricity, the supply-demand balance is likely to remain precarious in the future.

③ (イ) There is a limit to what the government can do to ensure a supply-demand balance if it only relies on saving power. It is essential to increase the supply capacity, but the assertions of the political parties do not convey a sense of urgency.

④ The parties have been generally in agreement on expanding renewable energy sources, such as solar power, in order to strike a balance between decarbonization and ensuring the supply of electricity.

⑤ However, renewable energy is not the key to maintaining a stable power supply because electricity generation from renewable energy sources is affected by the weather and the seasons. The supply-demand situation is projected to become even tighter this winter when solar power generation will decline.

⑥ (ロ) The Liberal Democratic Party has revised its previous policy of reducing the nation's dependence on nuclear power as much as possible and now states in its election pledge that the party will seek the maximum use of nuclear power generated at plants that have been confirmed to be safe. The LDP has made its stance to promote the restart of nuclear reactors clearer than before.

⑦ Komeito, the LDP's ruling coalition partner, has also put forth a policy of striving to restart nuclear reactors by obtaining public understanding and cooperation. Among the opposition parties, Nippon Ishin no Kai (Japan Innovation Party) and the Democratic Party for the People have accepted the restart of nuclear reactors that have been confirmed to be safe.

⑧ However, it is unclear (い) [   ] these parties will support the restart of the reactors.

⑨ Of the 27 reactors for which power companies have applied to the Nuclear Regulation Authority for safety screenings since the Great East Japan Earthquake, firms have managed to resume operations at least once for only 10 units. (う) Behind this slow progress is deep-rooted public distrust of nuclear power.

⑩ Efforts should be made to gain widespread understanding of the need for nuclear power. Another reason for the slow progress is the NRA's prolonged safety screenings. (え) [It is / There is / We are] hoped that the parties will discuss ways to speed up the process.

⑪ (ハ) In contrast, the Constitutional Democratic Party of Japan has been vague about its stance regarding the restart of nuclear reactors, while saying it does not approve of the construction of new reactors. The Social Democratic Party has called for moving away from the use of nuclear power, and the Japanese Communist Party has called for nuclear power to be abolished immediately.

⑫ If these parties reject the restart of nuclear reactors, they must devise effective alternative measures to achieve a stable electricity supply without nuclear power.

⑬ (お) Russia's invasion of Ukraine has made energy security even more important. How will resource-poor Japan cope with this situation? It is hoped that discussions on energy security will deepen during campaigning for the upper house election.

(July 4, 2022 | The Japan News)

power crunch 電力不足 / the House of Councillors election 参院選 / advisory［米話］注意報：a power crunch advisory で「電力需給ひっ迫注意報」/ Tokyo Electric Power Company Holdings, Inc. 東京電力ホールディングス株式会社 / precarious 不安定な / strike a balance between A and B A と B のバランスを保つ / decarbonization 脱炭素化 / election pledge 選挙公約 / ruling coalition 連立政権 / the Democratic Party for the People 国民民主党 / the Nuclear Regulation Authority 原子力規制委員会 / the Great East Japan Earthquake 東日本大震災 / the Constitutional Democratic Party of Japan 立憲民主党 / the Social Democratic Party 社民党 / the Japanese Communist Party 日本共産党 / resource-poor 資源の乏しい

Vocabulary Check

定義欄から適切なものを選んで単語の意味・内容を確認しておきましょう。

［単語］

　　1．scorching　2．ensure　3．surge　　4．unseasonably　5．conserve
　　6．convey　　7．pledge　8．confirm　9．resume　　　10．distrust

    a. not usually for the season

    b. to continue after interruption

    c. to bring about something

    d. doubt; a lack of trust

    e. to make something sure

    f. something promised

    g. to prove the truth of something

    h. very strong; hot enough to be burnt

    i. to be increased; to come about suddenly

    j. to keep something from being wasted

Stream of the Article

　この英文全体を読むと以下のような構成になります。記号（a）から（e）までの内容を記述して、この構成分析を完成させてください。

1. 電力不足の継続が懸念される中、（a　　　　）を戦う中で、各党は電力の安定供給の具体的な方策を提示することが急務となっている。

2. ６月下旬に、政府は、電力需給ひっ迫注意報を東京電力管内に初めて発令した。その理由は、季節外れの暑さのために電力の需要が高まることにある。政府は、（b　　　　）と企業の両方にエネルギー消費を抑えるよう要請した。

3. 民間の省エネに頼るだけでは、政府ができることが制限される。供給能力を高めることが極めて重要なのだが、各党の主張には緊迫感がない。

4. （c　　　　）などの代替エネルギーを推進することで、概ね各党は一致している。ところが、このエネルギーは安定した電力供給の維持のカギとならない。その理由として、代替エネルギーからの発電は、天気や季節に影響される。

5. 自民党は原子力にできるだけ頼らないというかつての方針を変更し、安全が確認されれば、できる限り原子力を使う方向を選挙の（d　　　　）に謳っている。

6. 自民党・日本維新の会・国民民主党は原子力を推進しているのに対し、（e　　　　）はスタンスが曖昧、社民党は原子力使用しない方向を目指し、共産党は即時廃止を求めている。

7. ロシアのウクライナ侵攻によりエネルギーの安全保障の問題がこれまで以上に深刻化し、参院選の選挙運動でその問題が議論されることが望まれる。

Interpretation and Translation ✏ 英➡日

1．③パラグラフの下線部（イ）の意味を日本語で表してください。

_____

_____

2．⑥パラグラフの下線部（ロ）の意味を日本語で表してください。

_____

_____

3．⑪パラグラフの下線部（ハ）の意味を日本語で表してください。

_____

_____

表現の泉

「頼る」の英語表現

　第 3 パラグラフに rely on という表現が出てきますが、「〜に頼る」という英語は、前置詞 on を伴うことが多いことに注目しましょう。on が接触して、寄りかかるイメージを持つので、このような意味になったと思われます。

depend on 〜，count on 〜，reckon on 〜，lean on 〜，fall back on 〜など

draw on 〜の場合は、「銀行の預金口座からお金を引き出す」という意味があり、そこから「〜を頼りにする」の意味が派生しました。

sponge on 〜は、「頼る」を通り越して、「〜にたかる」という意味が出ています。

He always sponges on his best friend.（彼はいつも親友にたかっている）

なお、「〜を頼りにする」という意味の表現で、on を用いない例も挙げておきます。

trust to 〜，resort to 〜，look / turn to 〜 for help

Grammar and Comprehension

1．（あ）の［　　］に入る単語の形のうち最も適切なのはどれですか。

  （A）business　（B）businesses　（C）business's　（D）businesses'

2．（い）の［　　］に当てはまる単語はどれですか。

  （A）how　（B）what　（C）which　（D）why

3．（う）の下線部は倒置文です。その元の形として正しいのはどれですか。

  （A）Behind this slow progress, public distrust of nuclear power is deep-rooted.

  （B）Deep-rooted public distrust is behind this slow progress of nuclear power.

  （C）Deep-rooted public distrust of nuclear power is behind this slow progress.

  （D）Slow progress is deep-rooted public distrust of nuclear power behind this.

4．（え）の［　　］内に当てはまる語句として正しいものを選んでください。

  ［　　　　　　　　　　　　　　］

5．（お）の下線部の表現と同じ意味となる構造を選んでください。

  （A）the invasion of Russia from Ukraine

  （B）the invasion of Ukraine into Russia

  （C）Ukraine's invasion by Russia

  （D）Ukraine's invasion of Russia

文法の小箱　　　　　　構造の理解

　第6パラグラフの最後の文、The LDP has made its stance to promote the restart of nuclear reactors clearer than before. を解説します。

　この文は第5文型で、S が the LDP、V が has made、O が its stance ... reactors、C が clearer than before となります。

　O の構造は、its stance を to promote の不定詞句が修飾していて、promote の目的語が the restart of nuclear reactors です。restart the nuclear reactors（動詞句）を名詞化して、the restart of nuclear reactors となっています。

　この文の訳例は「自民党は原子力の反射炉の再稼働を推進する立場をこれまで以上に明確化してきた。」となります。

Interpretation and Composition 🖊 日➡英

次の日本語を英語に訳してください。

1．聖武天皇は、743 年に国家鎮護を目指して、大仏建立の 詔 （みことのり） を発しました。

　　ヒント 詔を発する issue an Imperial edict

_____

_____

_____

2．聖徳太子は仏教の興隆が、健全な政治を推進する鍵であると考えました。

　　ヒント 〜の鍵である be the key to doing 〜

_____

_____

_____

深掘りの視点

代替エネルギーとは？

　石炭・石油・天然ガスなどの化石燃料は有限で、しかも温室効果ガスを出すとうマイナスの側面があるので、これに代わるエネルギーが代替エネルギーです。

　具体的には、太陽光・太陽熱・風力・地熱・バイオマスなどの再生可能エネルギーが代表的なものです。

　なお、太陽光発電は、太陽の光エネルギーを太陽電池により直接電気に変換して発電するシステムであるのに対し、太陽熱発電は、太陽光をレンズなどで集め、その熱で蒸気タービンを回して発電するという形をとります。

Spanish falcons feed Arab passion for raptor hunting
アラブ諸国が本気の鷹狩、スペインの鷹商人潤う！

⏸ 10

① For centuries, the art of falconry has been a prestigious tradition within Arab society. Today most of these formidable predators come from Spain, which has become the world's top exporter.

② In upper-class Gulf society, these swift-flighted hunters are worth a fortune, with buyers sometimes shelling out tens of thousands of euros per bird.

③ "The feathers must be completely whole," says Juan Antonio Sanchez, proudly showing off one of his falcons which is about to be shipped to Qatar.

④ Every year, around 150 of (あ) them leave the breeding facility that Sanchez runs with partner Beatriz Dominguez in Fuentespina in the arid Castille region, some 150 km north of Madrid. (い) [   ] Middle East, where rich amateurs buy them for race and hunt.

⑤ A breeder for more than 15 years, Sanchez and others helped turn Spain into the world's number one exporter of falcons in 2018, according to figures from the Convention on International Trade in Endangered Species (CITES).

⑥ (イ) Last year, Spain exported some 2,800 specimens, almost all of them to Gulf countries, easily passing the 2,500 sold by the U.K.

⑦ With 52 falcons due to be flown out the next day, Sanchez and Dominguez are making last-minute preparations for their journey.

⑧ With the help of two employees and their seven-year-old daughter, they take the birds out of the enclosures where they have been raised for the past three to five months, far from prying eyes.

⑨ The next day they will be loaded onto a lorry then transported to Madrid airport where, after passing veterinary checks and other formalities, they will be put on a plane to Qatar.

⑩ On the perches are a stunning array of hybrids. These particular ones were produced by crossing the gyr, the biggest and most elegant species of falcon, (う) with the peregrine, which is the fastest.

⑪ With their long, tapered wings, falcons have exceptional flight capabilities. The peregrine is known as the world's fastest animal, with diving speeds of up to 300 kph.

⑫ "There is ₍ₑ₎ [　　　] designed to be like a bullet," Dominguez whispers in the darkness of the corridors leading to the breeding enclosures.

⑬ Each raptor is sold for anywhere from €400 (¥48,300) to "thousands", says Sanchez.

⑭ According to Manuel Diego Pareja-Obregon, who heads the Spanish Falconry Association (AECCA), buyers from the Gulf tend to pay about €2,000 (¥241,500) per falcon.

⑮ But for specimens from a handful of breeding facilities known for supplying Gulf royalty and their families, the price tends to be in the tens of thousands, says Javier Ceballos, a Spanish falconry expert.

⑯ Such birds are raised in customized air-conditioned facilities where their trainers come and select the best specimens.

⑰ Julio Cesar Perez Guerra spent three years in Abu Dhabi looking after falcons that belonged to one of the brothers of United Arab Emirates President Sheikh Khalifa bin Zayed Al-Nahyan.

⑱ "They don't allow even one falcon with a broken feather back in, and if it happens, there's a sharp reprimand for the falconer who is handling them."

⑲ ₍ₗₒ₎ Spain counts around 400 breeders, many of whom started during the financial crisis by studying the art of breeding online in order to make a living off of their passion, explains Pareja-Obregon.

⑳ Spain has an age-old tradition of falconry dating back to the Middle Ages when the Visigoths and the Arabs introduced it to the region.

㉑ Today, hunting with raptors, which has been recognized on UNESCO's list of intangible cultural heritage, is practiced by just over 3,000 people in Spain, the European country where the sport is most deeply rooted.

㉒ ₍ₕₐ₎ But for breeders, Spain has a key advantage: its hot, dry climate allows the gyrfalcons — which normally live in higher, colder latitudes — to become acclimatized to the hotter temperatures they will experience in the Gulf.

㉓ In the Middle East, authentic hunts that have been practiced for centuries by nomadic tribes have become increasingly rare.

㉔ These days, the wild quarry the falcons would have hunted such as the houbara bustard — a rare desert bird ₍ₒ₎ [what / where / which / whose] meat is prized as an aphrodisiac — is now almost extinct.

㉕ Instead, birds of prey are used more for racing — against the clock or in pursuit of a remote-controlled robot "prey" — drawing criticism from purists.

㉖ Although possessing a falcon is an ostentatious sign of wealth, the owners often lose interest in an individual bird after about a year, heading back to the market in search of a new champion.

㉗ And this has provided a lucrative source of income for Spanish breeders that is showing little sign of letting up. (November 1, 2019 | The Japan Times alpha delivered by AFP-JIJI)

raptor 猛禽類 / falconry 鷹狩り / predator 捕食動物 / specimen 個々の（鳥）/ prying eye 詮索の目 / perch 止まり木 / array 勢ぞろい / gyr (gyrfalcon) シロハヤブサ / peregrine ハヤブサ / supplying Gulf royalty and their families 王室と一族の必要を満たす / reprimand 叱責 / Visigoths 西ゴート族 / cold(er) latitude 寒帯地方 / nomadic tribe 遊牧民 / quarry 獲物 / houbara bustard フサエリショウノガン / aphrodisiac 媚薬 / purist 純粋主義者

Vocabulary Check

定義欄から適切なものを選んで単語の意味・内容を確認しておきましょう。

[単語]

　　1．formidable　　2．swift-flighted　　3．shell out　　4．arid　　5．head for ～

　　6．stunning　　7．acclimatize to ～　　8．ostentatious　　9．lucrative　　10．let up

[定義欄]

　　a. attractive; displaying

　　b. quite attractive

　　c. extremely dry

　　d. speedily flying

　　e. accustom to ～

　　f. to spend money needed

　　g. profitable

　　h. to go to ～

　　i. to be reduced in intensity or strength

　　j. causing fear

Stream of the Article

　この英文全体を読むと以下のような構成になります。記号（ a ）から（ e ）までの内容を記述して、この構成分析を完成させてください。

1．何世紀もアラブ諸国は鷹狩が盛んだ。
2．上流階級では大金を払ってもハヤブサ（狩り用の鷹）を手に入れたがる。
3．Sanchez 氏とその仲間は（a　　　　　）を世界一のハヤブサ（狩り用の鷹）を輸出する国にした。
4．商品（鷹）の扱いには細心の注意を払う必要がある。
5．体格がよく優美な（b　　　　　）とハヤブサ（peregrine）を掛け合わせたハイブリッドも作り出している。
6．Gulf（湾岸）諸国からの買い手は鳥に（c　　　　　）ユーロ程のお金を払う。
7．もともとスペインには（d　　　　　）の伝統があり、それをアラブ人や西ゴート族が取り入れた。
8．これら猛禽類は今日では狩りではなく（e　　　　　）に使われている。
9．富裕層は一羽の鳥には飽き足らず次から次に別の鳥を買い求める。
10．おかげでスペインの鳥販売ビジネスは繁盛している。

Interpretation and Translation 🖉 英➡日

1．⑥パラグラフの下線部（イ）の意味を日本語で表してください。

_____

_____

2．⑲パラグラフの下線部（ロ）の意味を日本語で表してください。

_____

_____

3．㉒パラグラフの下線部（ハ）の意味を日本語で表してください。

_____

_____

Birds in their little nests agree.「小さな巣の鳥たちは仲がいい」

bird という単語は OE や ME（古代英語・中世英語）では bridd、brid または bird と綴られていました。語源の詳細は不明ですが、古くから英語の語彙に存在しています。

bird の意味は種々あります。英語で示すと以下のようになります。

a game bird / a fellow / a peculiar person / a young girl

a game bird「狩猟鳥」という名称は知られていても（日本語では）この表現はあまり使わないようです。「相手に襲いかかる鳥（猛禽）」は birds of prey と表現します。例として hawk, falcon, vulture などがあります。

古英語時代からの単語なので諺にも使われたものが多くあります。以下に示します。

Birds in their little nests agree. →「狭い共同体は仲がいい」と肯定的なもの、「なれ合い」とか「小さな共同体では和の精神がはびこる」と否定的なもの、どちらにも解釈できます。

The crow thinks her own bird fairest. →「カラスは自分の子供が一番いいと思っている」「親ばか」「身内をかばいすぎ」などの意味。

It's an ill bird that fouls its own nest. →「巣をダメにするのは悪い鳥」「立つ鳥あとを濁さず」と教訓的な解釈もされます。

Kill two birds with one stone. →「一石二鳥」とおなじみの表現ですが、これは英語から日本語に入った「翻訳のことわざ」です。

Grammar and Comprehension

1．（あ）の them が指しているものを選んでください。

   （A）formidable predators   （B）buyers in upper-class Gulf society

   （C）Sanchez's falcons   （D）tens of thousands of euros

2．（い）の［   ］内に入れるのに文法的・文脈的に最適な語句を選んでください。

   （A）Most head for the   （B）The most for head

   （C）The head most for   （D）Head most for the

3．（う）の下線部の語句が修飾している箇所を下から選んでください。

   （A）were produced   （B）crossing

   （C）species of falcon   （D）which is the fastest

4．（え）の［   ］に入れるのに文法的・文脈的に正しい表現を選んでください。

   （A）no one part of their bodies that is no

   （B）no parts of their bodies that is not

   （C）not more part of their bodies that is not

   （D）not one part of their bodies that is not

5．（お）の［　　　］の関係詞のうち最も適切なものを選んでください。
　　　［　　　　　］

文法の小箱

構造の理解

　第9パラグラフの文、The next day they will be loaded onto a lorry then transported to Madrid airport where, after passing veterinary checks and other formalities, they will be put on a plane to Qatar. を解説します。

　then 以下の transported to ... は、その直前の loaded onto a lorry に対応しています。where の先行詞は Madrid airport で、固有名詞なので元来 where は非制限用法で用いられるべきですが、時事英語ではコンマを用いない例が増えてきています。after passing ... formalities は where 節内への挿入節です。

　この文の試訳は「次の日、その鳥はローリーに積み込まれ、マドリード空港に輸送され、そこで、獣医学上の検査と他の手続きを済ませたあと、カタールへの飛行機に乗せられます。」となります。

Interpretation and Composition ✐ 日➡英

以下の日本語をよく読んで、下線部のみを通訳してください。

1．Still water runs deep という英文のことわざがある。たいていの場合はこの日本語訳は「能ある鷹は爪を隠す」となっている。しかし「わめかない」「さわがない」のが賢者の印という日本的解釈は英語のことわざにないようだ。米国では政治家でもコマーシャルでも機関銃のようにまくしたてることが「頭が切れる」という印象を与えるようだ。

　　ヒント わめく clamor, shout noisily ／さわぐ make a fuss, fuss ／機関銃のようにまくしたてる talk like a machine-gun, do a machine-gun talking

---

2．そもそも鷹狩りというのは北東アジアや沿海州が起源だが、鷹は人工孵化が出来ないのが難点である。そこで幼鳥を手に入れて育てながら技を仕込むのだそうだ。日本では山や地名に鷹という言葉がつくものがあれば、それは鷹の幼鳥を確保するための保護区域の名残の可能性が高い。

ヒント 幼鳥 young bird ／保護区域 sanctuary, protected area

深掘りの視点

鷹とは？

　タカ目タカ科に属する鳥のうち、比較的小さなものを指す通称です。比較的大きいものをワシ（鷲）と呼んでいます。

　縄文時代の遺跡からタカの骨が発見されていて、人間の食料であったようです。しかし、現代では、飼いならした鷹を野山に放って行う狩猟、すなわち、鷹狩り（falconry）が知られています。なお、ハヤブサ目ハヤブサ科の鳥を使った場合も、鷹狩りと言います。

　ちなみに、鷹の糞は、平安時代の医薬書『本草和名』（ほんぞうわみょう）に医薬品として記載されています。

経済

11 French restaurants are open but short-staffed
フランスのレストランは営業していて、
しかも人手不足？

⏐⏐ 11

① French restaurants are open but short-staffed. Even in gastronomy's capital, waiters and chefs have lost their taste for the job.

② (あ) [　　　　] to find extra staff, the manager of a bar in the Paris region recently asked her sister to drive for an hour to help out on a busy evening, during a televised football match. At a Normandy sea-front restaurant, a waitress says they are under-staffed because former colleagues will no longer put up with unsociable evening and weekend work. (イ) Diners in Paris report the sudden appearance of shorter menus, as restaurants adapt their kitchens to staff shortages, as well as the presence of improbably young (and ungrumpy) fresh recruits now waiting tables *en terrasse*.

③ Two months (い) [after / later] France reopened outdoor dining, restaurants and bars face a staffing crunch. (ロ) The share of hospitality firms reporting recruitment problems doubled in June from the previous month, according to a Bank of France survey. When restaurants and hotels were closed for months during lockdown, many former staff acquired a taste for normal family life, says Julia Rousseau, head of Éthique RH, a recruitment consultancy. She now sees candidates (う) [　　] alternative careers, as estate agents or in banks. "The pandemic has reordered their priorities," she says.

④ Hospitality is not the only sector with this trouble. In June 44% of all firms reported recruitment problems, (え) [while / with] the figure rising to 50% for construction work. "The bottleneck for French growth in mid-2021", wrote François Villeroy de Galhau, governor of the Bank of France, earlier this month, is "the reappearance, already, of hiring difficulties." France's case is particularly striking because its unemployment rate, at 7.5%, is higher than the OECD average (though lower than that of the euro area). Firms face labour shortages even as 2.4m people are officially looking for work.

⑤ Even before the pandemic, this gap was a worry. The government had been trying to close it with extra apprenticeships and training schemes. Now these have been expanded, with a more active approach to getting young people in particular into work. A scheme known as "One youth, one solution" guarantees every under-26-year-old training, an apprenticeship or a job, for which firms may get a public subsidy. The poorest get nearly €500 ($590) extra in benefits a month if they enrol in an active job-hunt scheme. "The government has invested a lot in upskilling," says Ludovic Subran, chief economist at Allianz, an insurer. "But there's an underlying mismatch between supply and demand that will remain for some time."

⑥ In parallel, there is an attempt to redesign the unemployment-benefit rules to encourage people to work. _(ハ) President Emmanuel Macron's reform involves, among other things, curbing the generous pay-outs to high-earners while also increasing from four to six months the length of service required to qualify for full benefits. This latter measure is designed to discourage firms from creating short-term contracts, which they do knowing that people can fall back on benefits in between. But after unions took the reform to France's highest administrative court, the government was told in June to suspend _(お) it until the economy improves. Mr. Macron vows it will apply from October, if growth picks up.

⑦ Staff shortages in the hospitality business may be linked to its generous furlough schemes. This will be tested at the end of August, when such workers will get only 72% of salaries rather than 84%. That may help firms entice staff back. So might better pay. For the moment, as restaurants prepare to check vaccination passes at entry, uncertainty is discouraging them from promising higher wages. Diners may need to get used to longer waits, and fewer alternatives to the *plat du jour*. (July 24, 2021 ｜ The Economist)

---

gastronomy 美食、調理 / colleague 職場の同僚 / (real) estate 不動産 / bottleneck 邪魔、阻害要因 / apprenticeship 実習生や見習い職人としての資格 / scheme 計画、企画 / parallel 平行、平行線 / furlough 一時休暇 / entice = to tempt to lure / wages 賃金 / plat du jour（その日の）特別料理

Vocabulary Check

定義欄から適切なものを選んで単語の意味・内容を確認しておきましょう。

[単語]

1. under-staffed　2. improbably　3. alternative　4. reorder　　5. striking
6. expand　　　7. underlying　8. curb　　　9. fall back on　10. suspend

[定義欄]

a. badly impressive　　　b. another　　　c. short of workers

d. to an unlikely degree　　e. to continue; not to end

f. to become or make ～ more in size and degree　g. to check or restrain

h. being the basis of ～ or supporting ～ from beneath

i. to rearrange　　　　　j. to come to depend on something as last resort

Stream of the Article

　この英文全体を読むと以下のような構成になります。記号（a）から（e）までの内容を記述して、この構成分析を完成させてください。

1．現状＝「料理人たちは仕事が嫌になった」
　　具体例（1）：パリとノルマンディーでの人手不足。
　　具体例（2）：パリではレストランの（a　　　　　）が短くなった。
2．人手不足の現状分析
　　接客業界の現状
　　具体例：人手不足で悩む接客業の割合は（b　　　　　）した。
　　理由：家族と過ごす普通の生活のほうがいい。
3．フランス経済の発展のためには
　　（1）再び（c　　　　　）がその邪魔をしている。
　　（2）しかし失業率は高いままだ。
4．フランス大統領の政策
　　（1）高収入者の失業手当を（d　　　　　）する。
　　（2）失業手当受給資格の厳格化。
5．当面の見込みは
　　（1）レストランでは食事客の列は長い。
　　（2）（e　　　　　）以外のメニューはますます選択肢が限られてくる。

Interpretation and Translation 英➡日

1．②パラグラフの下線部（イ）の意味を日本語で表してください。

_____

_____

2．③パラグラフの下線部（ロ）の意味を日本語で表してください。

_____

_____

3．⑥パラグラフの下線部（ハ）の意味を日本語で表してください。

表現の泉	英語に入った外国語

　英語に流入したフランス語経由の食事関係の単語を見てみると以下のようになります。日本でもおなじみの英語名称ももとは外来語であったことがわかります。

　魚介類では salmon（鮭）、sardine（いわし）、oyster（かき）など。鳥類は poultry（家禽）、pigeon（若鳩）など。食肉では venison（鹿肉）、beef（牛肉）、mutton（羊肉）、pork（豚肉）などがありますが、これらは料理用語です。

　これらを飼育している段階の名称は英語が使用されました。deer（鹿）、ox（牛）、calf（仔牛）、sheep（羊）swine / pig（豚）など。これらはすべてゲルマン系（古英語）の言葉であり、宮廷貴族が食卓に料理された肉を食する時はフランス語（英語話者にとっては外国語）の表現を用いました。これらの単語に関して、ドイツ語やフランス語の場合は、食卓の料理のみを外国語で表すことはあまりありません。

　そのほか、sherbet（シャーベット）、sugar（砂糖）、olive（オリーブ）なども外来語として英語に入ってきましたが、これらはそれぞれ、アラビア語起源、サンスクリット語起源、ギリシャ語起源です。

　デザート類はさらにおなじみの名前が続きます。almond（アーモンド）、raisin（レーズン、）fig（イチジク、）orange（オレンジ）、grape（グレープ）、lemon（レモン）、cherry（チェリー）、peach（ピーチ）など。これらも主としてフランス語経由で英語に入った外来語です。

Grammar and Comprehension

1．（あ）の［　　］に当てはまる最も適切な単語を選んでください。
　（A）Struggle　（B）Struggled　（C）Struggling　（D）A struggle

2．（い）の［　　］に当てはまる単語のうち正しいほうを選んでください。
　［　　　　　　　　］

3．（う）の［　　］に当てはまるのに最も適切な単語を選んでください。
　（A）seeks　（B）sought　（C）to seek　（D）seeking

4．（え）の［　　］に当てはまる単語のうち正しいほうを選んでください。
　［　　　　　　　　］

5.（お）の下線部 it が指しているものを選んでください。

（A）President Emmanuel Macron's reform

（B）France's highest administrative court

（C）a policy of creating short-term contracts

（D）the improvement of economy in France

文法の小箱

構造の理解

　第6パラグラフ第3文、This latter measure is designed to discourage firms from creating short-term contracts, which they do knowing that people can fall back on benefits in between. の解説をします。

　discourage O from doing ... で「O に…する気をなくさせる」、which の先行詞は、creating short-term contracts と考えられ、これが which they do の do の内容となります。they とは firms のことで、knowing の意味上の主語は、they（＝ firms）です。

　この部分の箇所の試訳は「この後者の方法（＝ Macron's reform）は企業に短期契約をしないようにさせるために考えられたもので、実際、企業はそのようにしてきた。というのは、[そうすることで] 人々は仕事のない期間（＝ in between）の手当てに頼ることができると知っているからである。」となります。

Interpretation and Composition 🖊 日➡英

　以下の日本語をよく読んで、下線部のみを通訳してください。

1．食事でいえば京都は薄味の本場だが、戦国武将の織田信長は「薄味」がどうしても嫌いで、この嗜好を身につけようとはしなかった。油を使い甘味のきいた食事を好んだのは、しっかり食べて天下取りのために体力を維持することが必要だったからだ。

　ヒント 薄味の spice-free ／どうしても obstinate enough ／身につける acquire

_____

_____

_____

2. ところで米軍だが、ベトナム戦争ではヘリコプター部隊でジャングルに食事を落下させていった。取り出して「すぐに食べられる」というのが一番だというので、即席麺が活躍したが、だんだんと「時にはビフテキも食べたい」し「食後はコーヒーも飲みたい」ということになった。実のところ食は戦士の士気に大きく影響する。

> **ヒント** 一番 priority ／取り出す yank ／だんだんと〜になる gradually transform

---

深掘りの視点

フランス語流入の歴史

　英語は語彙に関する限りフランス語の影響を大きく受けています。英国の一流のレストランではメニューはフランス語で書かれている場合が多くありますが、これには歴史的経緯があります。

　1066 年（日本では平安時代の前九年の役がおさまったころ）にフランスのノルマン地方の王（William 征服王）が英国の王位継承権を主張したことがもとで、英国侵攻（The Norman Conquest）が始まりました。これがフランス語流入のはじまりです。

　ドーバー海峡に面したハスティング（Hasting）の戦いでノルマン側が勝利しましたが、その後も戦いは続き、英国の諸侯はほとんどが没落しました。それ以降 300 年近くフランス語が英国の公用語になります。英語が公用語として再び姿を現すのは 1362 年（日本では足利尊氏から義満のころ）です。

　はじめのうちフランス語の流入は、宮廷・軍・司法などの関係に限られていましたが、1250 年ごろからは支配者（ノルマン人）と被支配者（土着の英国人）の融合が進み、膨大な数のフランス語が流入します。1066 年以降の英国において、支配者はフランス語を使用して、被支配者は英語を使用することになったのです。

　つまり英国は二重言語（social bilingualism）の国になりました。宮廷貴族はフランス語で会話し、英国王は英語の話せない状態が続きました。軍隊もフランス語で指揮され、裁判もフランス語で行われました。

　いまでも英国で最も人気のある英国王の一人リチャード獅子王（Richard the Lion-Hearted 1199 年没）も在位期間（およそ 10 年）で英国にいたのは半年ほどです。偶然ながら、獅子王と源頼朝の没年が重なります。リチャードは武勇に優れ第三回十字軍では特に勇名をはせました。彼もフランス語を使用し、英語は話しませんでした。

科学

12 COVID air war being lost, experts warn, urging mass ventilation
換気の重要性

🔊 12

① The world is still not using one of its most effective weapons against COVID-19 — properly ventilating public spaces — more than two years into the pandemic, experts warn.

② At the moment there is a "fragile, armed peace" with COVID-19, said Antoine Flahault, director of the Institute of Global Health at the University of Geneva.

③ "In the hopes of stemming the tide of the pandemic and reducing mortality, we need to reduce the level of contamination, (あ) which the vaccine cannot do alone," he said.

④ "We need a new phase — improving the quality of indoor air."

⑤ COVID-19 is primarily transmitted through the air. It is carried in large droplets or fine aerosols when an infected person breathes — and even more so when they talk, sing or shout.

⑥ In a closed off or (い) [   ] room, these aerosols can remain in the air for some time, moving around the space and greatly increasing the risk of infection.

⑦ While it is generally accepted that COVID-19 can be transmitted within 2 meters (6.5 feet) via both droplets and aerosols, there is still no consensus on the importance of long-distance airborne transmission indoors.

⑧ A team of researchers from the U.K. Health Security Agency and the University of Bristol reviewed 18 studies in several countries on airborne transmission.

⑨ In research published in the BMJ this week, they found that people can infect each other when they are more than 2 meters apart.

⑩ We know one thing for sure: If you open a window, or well-ventilate a space, the virus-carrying aerosols dissipate like smoke.

⑪ (イ) But experts say that nowhere near enough is being done to ventilate public and private spaces across the world.

⑫ "On the whole, this is an issue that governments have not yet taken up," Flahault said.

⑬ He called for massively increased funding to ventilate many public spaces, starting with schools, hospitals, public transport, offices, bars and restaurants.

⑭ "Just as we knew to filter and treat drinking water" in homes at the beginning of the 1900s, "(う) one can imagine some households will equip themselves with air purifiers and consider opening their windows," Flahault said.

⑮ Only a few countries have announced ventilation plans (え) [   ] the start of the pandemic.

⑯ In March, the U.S. government called on all building owners and operators, as well as schools and universities, to "adopt key strategies to improve indoor air quality."

⑰ The plan, dubbed the Clean Air in Buildings Challenge, is covered by previously announced COVID-19 funding and also includes a review of existing ventilation, heating and air conditioning systems.

⑱ The European Union has not issued any binding statements on improving air quality in light of COVID-19.

⑲ However, (ロ) Belgium has announced a plan to have a carbon dioxide meter situated in all places open to the public. Having such a meter is voluntary until the end of 2024, (お) when it becomes mandatory.

⑳ Stephen Griffin of the School of Medicine at Britain's University of Leeds lamented that the U.K. had not acted more on ventilation.

㉑ "(ハ) Sadly, the U.K. has not embraced the opportunity to safeguard its citizens in public spaces, its children in schools, or the longevity of the vaccination program in this way," he told the Science Media Center.

㉒ He said that setting minimum safety standards for ventilation in public buildings would also "greatly mitigate the impact of other diseases."

㉓ "Better ventilation also improves cognition by reducing carbon dioxide levels and, along with filtration, can reduce the impact of pollen and other allergies."

(July 22, 2022 | The Japan Times delivered by AFP-JIJI)

COVID-19 新型コロナウイルス感染症（coronavirus disease 2019 の略）/ the Institute of Global Health at the University of Geneva ジュネーブ大学グローバルヘルス研究所 / aerosol エアロゾル / airborne transmission 空気伝染 / the U.K. Health Security Agency 英国保険安全保障庁 / the University of Bristol ブリストル大学 / BMJ 英国医事ジャーナル（British Medical Journal の略）/ air purifier 空気清浄機 / in light of 〜 〜の観点から / the School of Medicine at Britain's University of Leeds 英国リーズ大学医学部 / the Science Media Center サイエンスメディアセンター：日本の一般社団法人（Science Media Centre と綴ればイギリスの会社）/ pollen 花粉

Vocabulary Check

定義欄から適切なものを選んで単語の意味・内容を確認しておきましょう。

[単語]

　　　1．pandemic　2．stem　　3．mortality　　4．droplet　5．dissipate
　　　6．massively　7．funding　8．mandatory　9．lament　10．mitigate

［定義欄］

  a. the ratio of deaths to population

  b. to express deep sorrow

  c. a tiny drop

  d. to make something less severe

  e. to vanish; to be scattered

  f. obligatory; authoritatively commended; officially required to do something

  g. an act of providing a sum of money for a certain purpose

  h. largely; greatly

  i. epidemic over a large region, especially across the world

  j. to stop something

深掘りの視点

公共の乗り物と換気

　航空機では、約３分で機内の空気がすべて入れ替わります。病院の手術室の空調設備にも使用されているフィルターを利用して、客室内に新しい空気が提供されるシステムとなっているのが普通です。空気は、天井から供給され、床下へ流れます。

　新幹線では、約６〜８分で空気がすべて入れ替わるように設計されています。床下の空調装置を通し、上へと空気が流れ、循環したのち、床下にある換気装置で車外へ流れるようになっています。

　路線バスの場合は、窓を閉めていても（夏の暑い時期）、約３分で空気を入れ替えることができます。ドアの開閉時などは自然に換気がされますが、長時間の旅行でドアの開閉が頻繁でない観光バスでも約５分で空気が入れ替わるような設計がなされています。

Stream of the Article

　この英文全体を読むと以下のような構成になります。記号（a）から（e）までの内容を記述して、この構成分析を完成させてください。

1．新型コロナウイルス感染症対策として最も効果的な武器を、世界はまだ使用していない。その武器とは、（a　　　　　）。パンデミックに突入して２年以上経っているのに…と専門家は警告する。

2．この汚染のレベルを下げるのに、（b　　　　　）だけでは十分とは言えない。屋内の空気の質を改善することが望まれる。

3．2m 以内の（c　　　　　）やエアロゾルで感染することは一般に理解されているが、長距離の空気伝染の重要性については、意見が分かれている。

4．世界中で、公的・私的スペースともに換気が十分とは言えない。ジュネーブ大学のFlahault 氏が要求しているのは、まず、学校・病院・（d　　　　　）・会社・バー・レストランの換気対策の資金を増やすこと。

5. 3月には、アメリカ政府は、屋内の空気の質を改善する方策を採用するよう、学校や大学はもちろん、すべてのビルの所有者・経営者に求めた。

6. EU は特に、空気の質改善に関する拘束力のある声明は出していないが、（e　　　　　）は、二酸化炭素メーターを公共のスペースに設置する計画を表明した。UK については、残念ながら、換気対策は十分とは言えない。

Interpretation and Translation 🖋 英➡日

1. ⑪パラグラフの下線部（イ）の意味を日本語で表してください。

_____

_____

2. ⑲パラグラフの下線部（ロ）の意味を日本語で表してください。

_____

_____

3. ㉑パラグラフの下線部（ハ）の意味を日本語で表してください。

_____

_____

表現の泉

「緩和する」の英語

　第 22 パラグラフに mitigate（緩和する）という単語が出てきますが、「緩和する」を意味する単語にはいろいろあります。目的語とともに、いくつか挙げます。

ease financial strain（財政緊縮を緩和する）

lighten the difficulty of living（生活難を緩和する）

lessen the severity of training（修業の厳しさを緩和する）

loosen a regulation（規制を緩和する）

alleviate inflation（インフレを緩和する）

relieve the pain（痛みを緩和する）

defuse tension（緊張を緩和する）

de-escalate an oil crisis（石油危機を緩和する）

moderate the speed of the car you drive（あなたが運転する車の速度を緩める）

Grammar and Comprehension

1．（あ）の which が指していることは何ですか。
　　（A）contamination　　　　　　　　（B）the level of contamination
　　（C）reduce the level of contamination　（D）need to reduce the level of contamination

2．（い）の［　　］に「換気がよくない」という意味の表現を入れるとしたら、どれが一番
　適切ですか。
　　（A）poor ventilating　（B）poorly ventilating
　　（C）ventilated poor　（D）poorly ventilated

3．（う）の one の意味として適切なのはどれですか。
　　（A）God　（B）people　（C）one person　（D）the same

4．（え）の［　　］に当てはまる単語はどれですか。
　　（A）from　（B）since　（C）until　（D）unless

5．（お）の when についての文法的情報として正しいものはどれですか。
　　（A）等位接続詞　（B）従位接続詞　（C）疑問副詞　（D）関係副詞

文法の小箱

旧情報と新情報

　一般に、SVO は「S は O を V する」と日本語に訳せます。主語は話題（＝相手が知っている情報＝旧情報）となるのが普通だからです。話題は「は」でマークされます。だから、John loves Mary は通常「ジョンはメアリーを愛している」となり、新情報をマークする「が」を用いた「ジョンがメアリーを愛している」は不自然なのです。一方、目的語は新情報（＝相手が知らないこと→言いたいこと）になる場合が多いと言えます。

　一般に、名詞句の場合、不定冠詞は新情報を表し、定冠詞は旧情報を表します。だから、文脈がない場合、例1が自然で、例2は不自然な英文です。

　例1：The man met a girl.（その男性はある少女に出会った。）

　例2：A man met the girl.（ある男性がその少女に出会った。）

　主語でも定冠詞をつけない（＝大半は新情報）ほうが自然な場合は、主語となる新たな情報を導入する場合や、一般論を述べる場合です。本文の例を挙げると…：

　例3：第8パラグラフ A team of researchers ...（ある研究者のチームが…）

　例4：第23パラグラフ Better ventilation also improves ...（よりよい換気はまた…）

例4のように、抽象名詞は無冠詞です。これは、「そんなよりよい換気」（=the better ventilation）という限定されたもの（＝先に述べた情報＝旧情報）ではないけれども、新情報とも言い切れません。それ故、「〜は」が自然です。このような一般論的陳述は、文全体で、新情報を述べていると言ってよいでしょう。

Interpretation and Composition ✏ 日➡英

次の日本語を英語に訳してください。

1. 日本では、クリスマスイブがクリスマスの前日であるという一般的見解がありますが、クリスマスイブとは、クリスマスの夕方という意味で、24日の日没より寝るまでの時間帯を言います。

   ヒント ～であるという一般的見解がある it is generally accepted that ～ ／～を言う referring to ～

   _____

   _____

   _____

2. 1228年、第3代執権北条泰時は、高野山の僧侶に対して、刀を持たないように要求しました。これが日本史記録上の初の刀狩りです。

   ヒント 執権 Regent ／～に対して…しないように要求する call on ～ not to do... ／刀狩り sword hunt, confiscation

   _____

   _____

   _____

UNIT

科学

13 Hydrogen goop could be a more convenient fuel than hydrogen gas
タンクに練り歯磨き？

13

① On paper, hydrogen looks like a dream fuel. Coal, oil and natural gas generate planet-warming carbon dioxide when burned. Hydrogen produces pure water. Hydrogen crams more energy into less space than batteries do (though, admittedly, less than petrol or diesel do). And an empty tank can be refilled with hydrogen much faster than an empty battery can be refilled with electricity.

② In practice, (あ) <u>things are trickier</u>. Storing meaningful quantities of hydrogen gas requires compressing it several hundred-fold. Liquefying it is another option, but (い) <u>one</u> that requires cooling the stuff to -253°C. Either process requires rugged tanks. Over time, hydrogen gas can infiltrate metals, weakening them and potentially causing cracks. Tanks must be built from special materials designed to resist this breakdown.

③ There may be a better way. Researchers at the Fraunhofer Institute for Manufacturing Technology and Advanced Materials in Germany, led by Marcus Vogt, think that supplying hydrogen as goop rather than gas offers a way around some of its limitations. (イ) <u>They have been experimenting with a chemical compound that can be pumped into a cartridge and then persuaded to give up its hydrogen on demand.</u>

④ Their invention, which they dub "Powerpaste," bears a passing resemblance to toothpaste. Its main ingredient is magnesium hydride, a compound that, when introduced to water, reacts with it to form hydrogen and magnesium hydroxide (a substance more familiar as milk of magnesia, a stomach-settling antacid). The escaped hydrogen can then be diverted into a fuel cell, where it reacts with oxygen from the air to generate electric power. The magnesium hydroxide waste is emptied from the reactor automatically.

⑤ Dr Vogt's scheme offers several advantages over batteries, petrol and more conventional ways of handling hydrogen. One is the storage of more energy per litre, and per kilogram, than either batteries or petrol can manage. A second is (う) [ ] of refilling, which is simply a matter of swapping an empty cartridge of paste for a full one, and topping up the water, which is stored in a separate tank. A third advantage is that, unlike a battery, the paste does not gradually lose its stored energy if it is left on the shelf.

⑥ (ロ) <u>Moreover, the paste itself is non-toxic, as are the reaction's by-products.</u> But there are plenty of subtleties to work through. Left to its own devices, magnesium hydroxide reacts only slowly with water because the reaction forms a barrier on the material's surface that inhibits further chemistry. To overcome this, Dr Vogt and his team have found a chemical additive that greatly accelerates the reaction. They have also found a way to ensure that the reaction can be controlled precisely enough to supply only as much hydrogen as is needed at any _(え) given moment.

⑦　_(ハ) The paste is unlikely to up-end the clean-car industry, where battery-powered vehicles have already established themselves as the dominant technology. But Dr Vogt nonetheless hopes that his invention may find niches. One early use could be in small vehicles such as scooters, or in flying drones _(お) where weight is at a premium. It is hard to scale down the sorts of heavy-duty tanks needed to store elemental hydrogen, he says. Powerpaste could thus enable longer ranges for scooters, and flight times for drones measured in hours rather than minutes. Miniature stoves aimed at campers are another idea.

⑧　A pilot plant in Brunswick, a city in Lower Saxony, will be able to produce four tonnes of the stuff per year when it is finished later this year. And heavier-duty uses are certainly possible, if that is what customers would like. Dr Vogt has already built a small demonstration unit for the German army.　　　(February 27, 2021 | The Economist)

---

carbon dioxide 二酸化炭素 / several hundred-hold 数百倍に / goop ペースト状のもの / magnesium hydride 水素化マグネシウム / magnesium hydroxide 水酸化マグネシウム / magnesia 酸化マグネシウム / antacid 酸中和剤、制酸剤 / subtleties 細部 / additive 添加物 / niches（業界の）隙間 / heavy-duty 丈夫な / elemental 基本的要素の、自然の / tonne［英］トン（＝ metric ton［1,000kg］）

Vocabulary Check

定義欄から適切なものを選んで単語の意味・内容を確認しておきましょう。

[単語]
　　1．cram　2．admittedly　3．liquefy　　4．rugged　5．infiltrate
　　6．dub　7．divert　　8．conventional　9．inhibit　10．accelerate

[定義欄]
　　a. to change into water-like substance　　b. to pass through into ～
　　c. to give title to ～; to name　　　　　　d. to make something happen more quickly
　　e. as an acknowledged fact　　　　　　　　f. to turn aside; to cause to go in another direction
　　g. to prevent; to check　　　　　　　　　h. traditional; following custom
　　i. to force ～ into small space　　　　　　j. strong; firm

Stream of the Article

　この英文全体を読むと以下のような構成になります。記号（a）から（e）までの内容を記述して、この構成分析を完成させてください。

1．水素の素晴らしさ＝夢の素材か？
　　具体例（1）：水素は純水（不純物のない水）を生み出す。
　　具体例（2）：（a　　　　　）。
2．問題点指摘
　　具体例（1）：水素ガスを保存するのに数百倍の圧縮を必要とする。
　　具体例（2）：（b　　　　　）。
　　→（1）と（2）のいずれの場合も、強靭なタンクが必要。
　　その理由：水素ガスは金属に浸透し、その金属を弱め、（c　　　　　）。
3．気体としてではなくペースト状のものが、問題解決の糸口発見となるか？
　　水素化マグネシウムを使用することで、電池・石油や水素を扱う伝統的な方法に比べて優っている点
　　利点（1）→エネルギーの蓄積量が増加する。
　　利点（2）→補充が簡単である。
　　利点（3）→（d　　　　　）。
4．ペースト状のもの自体の特長
　　無毒性
5．水酸化マグネシウムの問題点：反応速度が遅い
　　この問題の解消のために、2つのことを発見した。
　　（1）反応促進のための（e　　　　　）を発見した。
　　（2）反応の正確な制御を確実にする方法を発見した。
6．ペースト処理商品の見込み
　　（1）車業界は参入が難しい。
　　（2）業界の隙間を発見…たとえばスクーターなどの小型車やドローンなど。
7．ドイツ軍への商品サンプルの納入

③パラグラフの下線部（イ）の意味を日本語で表してください。

⑥パラグラフの下線部（ロ）の意味を日本語で表してください。

⑦パラグラフの下線部（ハ）の意味を日本語で表してください。

表現の泉	empty の語法

形容詞用法	制限用法　on an empty stomach（すきっ腹で）
	叙述用法　a house empty of furniture（家具がない家）
	※類似表現 void of 〜 / destitute of 〜 / barren of 〜
動詞用法	empty an ashtray（灰皿を空にする→灰皿の灰を捨てる）
	empty the glass of milk into a saucepan（その牛乳をシチュー鍋に移す）
	empty the water out of your boots（ブーツの水を取り除く）

Grammar and Comprehension

1. （あ）things are trickier の英文では比較級が使われています。than ～を付け加えるとしたら、以下の何が適切でしょうか？

   （A）than now　（B）than this　（C）than in practice　（D）than on paper

2. （い）one は代名詞ですが、どの名詞の代わりに使われていますか。

   （A）hydrogen gas　（B）liquifying　（C）option　（D）either process

3. （う）の［　　］に当てはまる単語はどれですか。

   （A）ease　（B）easy　（C）easily　（D）eased

4. （え）at any given moment の下線部の given と同じ用法である過去分詞（下線部）を含む文を、以下から選んでください。

   （A）Raised in the U.K., I understood why he spoke with strong British accent.

   （B）She was inclined to drinking when she ate a night meal.

   （C）The date of posting designated, I had prepared the document in advance.

   （D）I was deeply impressed with the conical mountain covered with snow.

5. （お）where weight is at a premium の英文を書き直した英文が以下に示されています。その英文の空欄を埋めるのにふさわしい単語を書き込んでください。

   where the (　　　) weight is, the better it is

文法の小箱　　　　　　構造の理解

　第4パラグラフ2行目、Its main ingredient is magnesium hydride, a compound that, when introduced to water, reacts with it to form ... を解説します。

　magnesium hydride の直後のコンマは、a compound 以下を指しています。このコンマは同格を表しています。when introduced to water は、a compound を先行詞とする関係節内に埋め込まれた節で、when it is introduced to water の it is が省略された形です。it は magnesium hydride を指しています。

　that は関係代名詞の主格で、対応する動詞句は reacts 以下で、with it の it は water を指しています。コンマ以下は、「水に触れたら（introduced）、それ（water）と反応し（react）…を生成する（form）ような化合物（compound）」の意味となります。

以下の日本語をよく読んで、下線部のみを通訳してください。

1. 水素エネルギーの話が出てきたころから技術部は色めき立ちました。日頃から経費無駄遣いの本丸扱いされていましたので、名誉挽回するチャンスとばかりに元気が出たのでしょう。水素を液化する技術に頼れば経営部門の問題まで解決できると考え、技術開発部は意気揚々と新技術を発表しました。

ヒント 経営部門の問題 managerial problems ／意気揚々とした exuberant, high-spirited

_____

_____

_____

2. しかし、ご存知のように、液化技術だけでは新しいよく売れる商品ができるかと言えば、そう単純でもない。技術部門も販売部門も知恵を絞り尽くすことが求められるわけで、生き残るためには現実的能力を可能な限り活用することが何にも増して重要なのです。

ヒント 知恵を絞る rack one's brains, think very hard ／現実的能力 savvy, practical knowledge

_____

_____

_____

深堀りの視点

水素エネルギーについて

　水素は、地球上で最も軽い気体で、その重さは、空気の約 14 分の 1 程度です。水素は酸素と反応させることで、電気と水が発生し、その電気をエネルギーとして利用できるのです。そのような水素エネルギーには、主に以下の 3 つの特徴があるとされています。
　（a）使うときに二酸化炭素が発生しない。
　（b）様々なものから生成できる。
　（c）エネルギーを水素に変えて保存できる。
　水素社会の実現を目指し、経済産業省は「水素・燃料電池戦略ロードマップ」を打ち出しました。下記の 3 つのフェーズが設けられました。
　フェーズ 1（2019 年〜）：燃料電池の社会への本格的実装段階。
　フェーズ 2（2020 年代半ば）：水素発電の本格導入、大規模な水素供給システムの構築。
　フェーズ 3（2040 年頃）：CO₂ フリー水素供給システムの確立。

科学

The science behind the first successful pig-to-human heart transplant
豚の心臓が人を救う！

It may lead to a new approach to organ transplantation

⫶|14

①　On January 7th David Bennett became the first person to have a heart (あ) [　　　] successfully into him from a pig. In press material issued three days after the operation, the University of Maryland confirmed Mr. Bennett was doing well, and was capable of breathing on his own. (イ) While he continues to rely on artificial support to pump blood around his body, the team behind the surgery, led by Bartley Griffith, plan gradually to reduce its use.

②　This operation is a milestone for xenotransplantation — the transfer of organs from other species to human patients. (い) It comes hot on the heels of another, in October, when a pig's kidney was successfully attached for three days to a brain-dead patient in a hospital in New York. On that occasion, mere surgical success was the goal. But Dr Griffith's team hope to save a life.

③　The operation itself received exceptional authorization from America's Food and Drug Administration under a provision which lets doctors use experimental treatments as a matter of last resort. Prior to it Mr Bennett was diagnosed with terminal heart disease, but was judged too ill to qualify for a human transplant. Having spent months in a hospital bed with no improvement to his condition, he gave his consent to the surgery.

④　The field's recent flowering has long-established roots. For decades, researchers have attempted to tackle xenotransplantation's fundamental problem. This is that the human body, when it recognizes foreign tissue, has a tendency to turn against it. In the case of pigs, the most important marker of foreignness is a sugar molecule called galactose-alpha-1,3-galactose (alpha-Gal), which is found on the surfaces of their cells. While this molecule does not exist in humans, antibodies to suppress it do. Consequently, no transplant from a pig with alpha-Gal would last more than a couple of minutes in a human body.

⑤　In 2003 pigs were produced with a genome modified so as to suppress the enzyme responsible for making alpha-Gal. This was a step in the right direction, but other barriers popped up in its place. (ロ) As Frank Dor of Imperial College, London, who was involved in that original genome-modification project, observes, with each of these barriers requiring years of work to overcome, many researchers — and much research funding — abandoned the field.

⑥　One collaboration which survived was that between the University of Maryland and Revivicor, a regenerative-medicine company in Blacksburg, Virginia. It was Revivicor that provided the genetically modified pig for Friday's surgery. The animal in question had a genome modified in ten ways, to optimize the chances of success. Three genes had been removed to reduce the risk of a human antibody (う) [　　　] the donor organ. A fourth, a growth gene, had also been knocked out, to ensure the heart did not enlarge after transplantation. And six human genes had been added, to promote acceptance.

⑦　In addition to the usual risks surrounding any heart transplant, there are a number of areas of concern that Dr Griffith and his colleagues will be looking out for. One is any hitherto-unknown rejection mechanism. Another is the possibility that the organ may transfer porcine viruses to its new host. The pig in question was reared in a sterile environment to minimize the chance of (え) that, but it remains a possibility.

⑧　Supporters of xenotransplantation think its potential to improve lives is huge. In America alone, over 100,000 people are waiting for transplants (though the vast majority need a kidney rather than a heart). In 2020 (お) [　　　] the required number of organs became available.

⑨　In theory, pigs can be bred to provide humans with any solid organ, though some will be more complex than others. A large part of the heart's function is mechanical, but other organs have chemical jobs that will be harder to replicate. (ハ) Moreover, even assuming these barriers can be overcome and successful surgical procedures developed, most researchers still acknowledge that scaling up xenotransplantation to meet the world's demand for organs may take decades. After this news, however, the chances that it will happen eventually have increased.

(January 15, 2022 | The Economist)

---

milestone 注目すべき業績 / xenotransplantation 異種間移植 / kidney 腎臓 / provision 条件、規定 / field 医学などの分野 / flowering 流行（隆盛）/ tissue 組織 / molecule 分子 / genome 遺伝情報 / enzyme 酵素 / antibody 抗体 / porcine 豚由来の / rear 育てる / replicate 複製する ［= to make a copy of ～］/ scale up 増加させる ［= to increase ～ in number］

Vocabulary Check

定義欄から適切なものを選んで単語の意味・内容を確認しておきましょう。

［単語］

1．confirm　　2．diagnose　　3．terminal　　4．qualify for　　5．regenerative
6．optimize　　7．knock out　　8．hitherto　　9．sterile　　　10．solid

［定義欄］

 a. completely clean   b. to make ～ as effective as possible

 c. having to do with replacing a body part by a new growth of tissue

 d. to find out what illness one has   e. up to this time

 f. to make sure   g. to remove

 h. dependable   i. resulting in death

 j. to ask for ～

Stream of the Article

　この英文全体を読むと以下のような構成になります。記号（a）から（e）までの内容を記述して、この構成分析を完成させてください。

1．豚から人への心臓移植成功
2．今回の実験的手法は（a   ）の手段として認められた。
3．移植手術の苦労と問題
4．今回の手術に向けての準備
5．再生医療業界との提携と工夫
　　A - 人間の側の抗体を抑えるためには（b ）を行った。
　　B - 豚の心臓の成長を抑えるためには（c ）を行った。
　　C - 臓器を受け入れやすくするためには（d ）を行った。
6．それでも移植手術のリスクは残る。
7．たとえ種々の問題点が克服されても、需要に応じるには（e ）の時間がかかる。
8．今後もこの種の移植手術が行われる可能性は高まった。

Interpretation and Translation 🖊 英➡日

1．①パラグラフの下線部（イ）の意味を日本語で表してください。

_____

_____

2．⑤パラグラフの下線部（ロ）の意味を日本語で表してください。

_____

_____

3．⑨パラグラフの下線部（ハ）の意味を日本語で表してください。

_____

_____

heart という言葉

heart という単語には「心」「臓器」「人柄」「記憶」「気力」「自信」「愛情」など多くの意味が込められています。

例1　A light purse makes a heavy heart.

「お財布が軽いと気持ちは重い」→この場合は「気分」の意味。

例2　Absence makes the heart grow fonder.

「顔を合わさなければより魅力を感じる」→この場合は「思いを募らせている人物」の意味になるでしょう。

例3　Far from eye, far from heart.

「会わないでいると、相手のことを忘れる」「去る者日々疎し」→この場合は「記憶」「思い出」の意味であり、heart の代わりに mind を使う場合もあります。

例4　Faint heart never won fair lady.

「気弱な男では美人はお付き合いしてくれない」→この場合は「人」「男」の意味。

Grammar and Comprehension

1．（あ）の［　　］に当てはまる語（句）として文法的に正しい形を下から選んでください。

（A）transplant　（B）transplanting　（C）transplanted　（D）to transplant

2．（い）の下線部の文において It と another は何を指していますか。下から正しい組み合わせを選んでください。

（A）It ＝ xenotransplantation / another ＝ another patient

（B）It ＝ a human organ / another ＝ another animal

（C）It ＝ a brain-dead patient / another ＝ another organ of a pig

（D）It ＝ a milestone / another ＝ another hospital in New York

3．（う）の［　　］に当てはまる語（句）として文法的に正しい形を下から選んでください。

（A）rejects　（B）rejecting　（C）rejected　（D）to reject

4．（え）の下線部 that が表している内容として最も適切な語句を選んでください。

(A) unknown rejection mechanism (B) the transfer of porcine viruses

(C) the pig in question (D) a sterile environment

5．（お）の［　　］に入れるのに文法的・文脈的に最も適切な語句を下から選んでください。

(A) the only third of (B) the only one third of

(C) only the third of (D) only a third of

文法の小箱　　　　　　　　強調構文が強調できないもの

It is X that .... の強調構文において、X が強調されています。この X の箇所に入れることができないものがあります。（1）動詞　（2）形容詞　（3）旧情報　（4）理由節は不可能です。

(1) × It is loves that John Mary.（×ジョンがメアリーをは愛するだ）

(2) × It is intelligent that Ann is.（×アンであるのは賢いだ）

(3) × It is since you love her that you should ask her out. ［since 節は旧情報を表す］

　　○ It is because you love her that you should ask her out. ［because 節は新情報を表す］

(4) × It is because he is staggering that he is drunk.（△彼が酔っているのはよろめいているからだ）

　　［because 節は、he is drunk が言える理由を表す節（＝理由節）となっている］

　　○ It is because he drank too much that he is drunk.（○彼が酔っているのは飲みすぎたからだ）

　　［because 節は、he is drunk の原因を表す節（＝原因節）となっている］

Interpretation and Composition 🖊 日➡英

以下の日本語をよく読んで、下線部のみを通訳してください。

1．幕末の安政 4 年（1857）にオランダから長崎に蒸気船が到着した。この船は後に咸臨丸という名で広く日本人に知られることになるが、ポンペ・ファン・メールデルフォールト（1829-1908）という名のオランダ人軍医が乗船していた。彼の長崎での活動は、外国語教育の面でも、医学教育の面でも、実に興味深い実例を残すことになった。

ヒント ポンペ・ファン・メールデルフォールト Pompe van Meerdervoort ／軍医 Army medic

2．このオランダ医師は、物理・化学・生物学・病理学・薬学・内科・外科を長崎で教えた。
几帳面な人で、ユトレヒトの軍医学校で学んだ際の講義録を保存しており、それを長崎
で再現して教えたらしい。まだ28歳の青年であった。それにしても、一人で西洋医学を
日本に移植しようというのである。講義はすべてオランダ語であった。学ぶほうの苦労
も想像にあまりある。

ヒント ユトレヒトの軍医学校 Imperial Academy for Military Medicine in Utrecht／講義録 lecture note

---

深掘りの視点

心臓について知る

　心臓がポンプの機能を持つことは誰でも知っていることですが、具体的に表現すると以下のようになります。
　(1) 1分間に5～6ℓの液体（血液）を送り出している。
　(2) 1時間で約300ℓの液体を送り出すことになる。
　これは家庭の風呂桶にためる水と同じくらいの分量。手作業でお風呂に水をためると重労働に感じます。それを心臓は休みなく行っています。
　また、心臓が単なるポンプと違う点は、その敏感で柔軟な対応能力です。たとえば、精神状態や臓器の状態、血液の必要性などで心臓は動きを調節して心拍数が大きく変動します。普通は、運動するとすぐに心拍数がそれに連動して変化します。
　人間の心臓は血液の逆流を防ぐ弁を持っていますが、これを調整しているのは筋（筋肉）です。僧帽弁や大動脈弁などもあり、全体で血流を調整しています。血管には次のような特徴もあります。
　(1) 人間の血管をすべてつないだ長さは10万キロに及ぶ。
　(2) 動脈は枝分かれを繰り返して細動脈になる。
　(3) 毛細血管では直径が1/20ミリのものもある。
　(4) 体の隅々まで血管網が行き渡っている。

●記事出典一覧

（各社の承諾を得て掲載しています）

第 1 章　What is intermittent fasting?
　　　　(July 8, 2022 ｜ Louise George Kittaka - The Japan Times alpha)
第 2 章　Viking era wooden sailboats make UNESCO's Heritage list
　　　　(February 11, 2022 ｜ The Japan times alpha delivered by AP)
第 3 章　Nigeria town celebrates claim as "twin capital" of world
　　　　(November 8, 2019 ｜ The Japan times alpha delivered by AFP-JIJI)
第 4 章　Artist adorns Egyptian cave church with biblical art
　　　　(August 16, 2019 ｜ The Japan times alpha delivered by AFP-JIJI)
第 5 章　Floating Fortress Musashi, symbol of Japan's naval ambitions, now a war grave
　　　　(March 16, 2015 ｜ The Japan Times)
第 6 章　Schools and Students look to boost youth voter turnout
　　　　(July 3, 2022 ｜ The Japan Times delivered by JIJI)
第 7 章　Restitution, But At What Price?
　　　　(December 14, 1998 ｜ TIME)
第 8 章　The New Testament's Unsolved Mysteries
　　　　(December 18, 1995 ｜ TIME)
第 9 章　Campaigning parties must present specific measures to boost power supply
　　　　(July 4, 2022 ｜ The Japan News)
第 10 章　Spanish falcons feed Arab passion for raptor hunting
　　　　(November 1, 2019 ｜ The Japan Times alpha delivered by AFP-JIJI)
第 11 章　French restaurants are open but short-staffed
　　　　(July 24, 2021 ｜ The Economist)
第 12 章　COVID air war being lost, experts warn, urging mass ventilation
　　　　(July 22, 2022 ｜ The Japan Times delivered by AFP-JIJI)
第 13 章　Hydrogen goop could be a more convenient fuel than hydrogen gas
　　　　(February 27, 2021 ｜ The Economist)
第 14 章　The science behind the first successful pig-to-human heart transplant
　　　　(January 15, 2022 ｜ The Economist)

重要単語リスト

intermittent	断続的な
involve	意味する、関係させる
approach	方法
remaining	残りの
go against 〜	〜に逆らう、〜に反する
ancestor	先祖
than ever	これまでになく、これまで以上に
stay up late	夜遅くまで起きている
challenging	難しい、やりがいのある
maintain	維持する
suit	〜に合う
night owl	夜型人間
fit into one's lifestyle	自らのライフスタイルに合う
agree with 〜	〜に同意する
recommend	推薦する

Intangible Cultural Heritage of Humanity	人類の無形文化財
designation	指定
exhibit	展示する
remains	遺物
archeological	考古学の
oversee	監督する
be characterized by	〜を特徴とする
longitudinal	縦長の、経度の
stuff	詰め込む
curator	（博物館の）館長
zenith	全盛期、絶頂
unsurpassed	上に出る者がない、卓越した
literally	文字通り
festivity	祭礼、祝祭
inscription	記載（刻まれたもの）、碑文

celebrate	祝う
elated	大喜びで、大得意で
identical (brother)	一卵性双生児の（兄弟）
outfit	服装一そろい

masquerade	仮装、仮面舞踏会
statistics	［複数扱い］統計、［不可算名詞］統計学
come by	手に入れる
gynecologist	婦人科医
epicenter	（問題などの）中心、震央
underway	進行中で
banish	追放する
contribute to	〜の原因となる、〜に貢献する
fertility	生殖、繁殖力、肥沃
skeptical	懐疑的である
consume	消費する

clamber up	よじ登る
carve	彫刻する
fulfil	（願望などを）満たす、（義務などを）果たす
miracle	奇跡
feat	偉大な業績
show off	〜を見せびらかす
recount	物語る、詳しく話す
allure	魅力、魅惑する
depiction	描写
pinnacle	頂上
artefact	美術品、工芸品［＝artifact］
accustomed to	〜に慣れて
command of	〜の言葉を自由に駆使できる力
autocrat	独裁者
turmoil	混乱

flagship	旗艦（きかん）、（同じ種類の中で）最高のもの
wreck	難破船
formidable	恐るべき、非常に優れた
obsolete	老朽化した
diameter	直径
specification	性能
critical	重要な、決定的な、批判的な
carrier aircraft	航空母艦
reluctant	気が進まない
deploy	配置する
lavish	贅沢な

put ~ in harm's way	～を危険な状況に晒す
torpedo	魚雷
doom	運命づける
prevail	優勢である

UNIT 6

boost	増加する、高める
turnout	投票者数
parliament	議会
participant	参加者
mock	模擬の
candidate	候補者
voting right	選挙権［＝suffrage］
law major	法学専攻の学生
hail from	～出身である
absentee ballot	不在者投票
distribute	配る
apply for	～を申し込む
specialize in	～を専門としている
procedure	手続き
constituency	選挙区

UNIT 7

privilege	特別（扱い）、特権、（特別な）名誉
live off ~	～で暮らしを立てる
siblings	兄弟姉妹
do time	刑期を務める
class action	集団訴訟
settle	解決する、同意に達する
confiscate	没収する
asset	資産
defamation	名誉棄損
attorney	法定代理人（弁護士）
roster	名簿
recourse	頼みの綱
subsidiary	子会社
sever	切り離す
contend	強く主張する、争う

UNIT 8

itenerant	巡回する
milieu	状況、環境
tantalize	じらして苦しめる
tenet	教義
ascetic	苦行者

oracle	神の言葉、神託
fervor	熱情
intriguing	興味深い
dedicate	～に捧げる、奉納する
speculate	（確実な根拠なしに）推測する
uncover	～の覆いをとる
validate	確証する、有効にする
devout	熱烈な、信心深い
testimony	証言
unearth	発掘する

UNIT 9

power crunch	電力不足
advisory	［米話］注意報
surge	急に高まる、上昇する
conserve	保存する
precarious	不安定な
decarbonization	脱炭素化
election pledge	選挙公約
ruling coalition	連立政権
confirm	確認する
resume	再開する
deep-rooted	根が深い
abolish	廃止する
reject	拒絶する
invasion	侵攻
resource-poor	資源の乏しい

UNIT 10

falconry	鷹狩り
predator	捕食動物
shell out	必要なだけの金を払う
arid	乾燥した、不毛の
specimen	見本、（動物の）標本
perch	止まり木
stunning	魅力的な、素晴らしい
head	～を統括する、～のリーダーである
reprimand	叱責
date back to	～に遡る
cold latitude	寒帯地方
acclimatized	順応した
ostentatious	見せびらかす、人目を引く
lucrative	儲かる
let up	静まる、弱まる

UNIT 11

gastronomy	料理法、食道楽
colleague	職場の同僚
put up with	～を我慢する
(real) estate	不動産
bottleneck	邪魔、阻害要因
apprenticeship	実習生や見習い職人としての資格
scheme	計画、企画
parallel	平行、平行線
curb	～を（強く）抑制する
discourage	やる気をなくさせる、思いとどまらせる
fall back on	～に頼る
furlough	一時休暇
entice	唆（そそのか）して～させる
wage	賃金
alternative	選択肢、代案

UNIT 12

COVID-19	新型コロナウイルス感染症（coronavirus disease 2019 の略）
pandemic	パンデミック（世界的流行病）
stem	くい止める、せき止める
mortality	死亡者数、死亡率
airborne transmission	空気伝染
dissipate	散る、消える
air purifier	空気清浄機
dub	～と称する
in light of ～	～の観点から
mandatory	義務的な、強制の
lament	悔やむ、嘆き悲しむ
embrace	取り入れる、喜んで応じる
safeguard	保護する
mitigate	緩和する、和らげる
pollen	花粉

UNIT 13

carbon dioxide	二酸化炭素
cram	詰め込む
admittedly	一般に認められているように、明らかに
liquefy	液化する

infiltrate	浸み込む、浸透する
divert	転換する、そらす
conventional	従来の、因習的な、型にはまった
subtleties	細部、微妙な点
inhibit	抑制する、防止する
additive	添加物
accelerate	速める、加速する
precisely	正確に
niches	（業界の）隙間
heavy-duty	丈夫な、非常に重要な
elemental	自然のままの

UNIT 14

milestone	注目すべき業績（金字塔）、画期的な事件
kidney	腎臓
provision	条件、規定
diagnose	診断する
flowering	流行（隆盛）
tissue	組織
molecule	分子
antibody	抗体
genome	遺伝情報
modify	修正する、（部分的に）変更する
enzyme	酵素
optimize	できるだけ効率的に利用する
rear	育てる
sterile	無菌の、殺菌した
minimize	最小限にする [↔ maximize]

重要例文集

1. Intermittent fasting doesn't tell you what foods to eat.
   断続的断食はどんな食べ物を食べるべきかを教えているのではない。

2. We stay up late eating snacks while using social media.
   我々はソーシャルメディアを利用しながら軽食を食べて遅くまで起きている。

3. All this makes it challenging to keep calorie count down.
   こんなことをしている限り、カロリー量を下げ続けるのは至難の業となる。

4. I'm a night owl and go to bed late.
   私は夜型人間で、寝るのが遅くなってしまう。

5. The most important thing is finding something that fits into your lifestyle.
   自分のライフスタイルにあったものを見つけることが肝心である。

1. The term "clinker" is thought to refer to the way the wooden boards are fastened.
   clinker という言葉はその木板の固定方法を指しているものと考えられている。

2. The museum not only exhibits the remains of vessels but works to rebuilt other boats.
   その博物館は船の残骸を展示するだけでなく、他の船の再建を目的として活動している。

3. The boats are characterized by the use of overlapping longitudinal wooden hull planks.
   その船の特徴は縦長の木製の厚板を重ねて使用することである。

4. It was during the Viking Age that clinker boats had their zenith.
   クリンカー船が全盛期を迎えたのはヴァイキング時代であった。

5. If you want to keep these skills alive, you have to keep them going.
   もしこのような技術を継承していきたいなら、その技術を使い続けなければならない。

1. The sleepy-looking town boasts of having the highest concentration of multiple births.
   その何の変哲もなさそうな町は多児分娩が最も集中して起こっていることが自慢である。

2. We feel elated that we are being honored today.
   今日は我々のことを尊重していただいているのですごく嬉しいです。

3. The whole world will better appreciate the importance of twins as gifts from God.
   全世界が神からの授かりものとしての双子の重要性を一層理解することになるだろう。

4. Igbo-Ora is the epicenter of the phenomenon in the West African country.
   イグボオラはその西アフリカの国において、その現象の中心地である。

5. That has not always been the case in parts of southern Nigeria.
   南ナイジェリアの各地で、昔からいつもそのようであったとは限らない。

1. I want you to turn the mountain into an open Bible.
   あなたにその山を開いた聖書のようにしていただきたい。

2. I had no idea sculpting was a talent I have but it tuned out to be as you can see.
   私に彫刻の才能があるなんて思いもしなかったのですが、見ての通りとなりました。

3. The story of moving the mountain is believed to have taken place in November, 979.
   その山を動かす話は、979 年 11 月に起こったものと信じられている。

4. It will benefit the people and create a lively depiction of these stories.
   そのことは人々のためになり、またこれらの話をありありと記述する世界を生み出す。

5. I just love living here. It's where I am most comfortable.
   私はここに住むのが大好きですが、ここが一番心が休まる場所です。

1. The news immediately made headlines in Japan.
   そのニュースは日本ではすぐにメディアで大きく報道された。

2. It was one of the two great battleships of the Imperial navy, the other being the Yamato.
   それは帝国海軍の 2 隻の大きな戦艦の 1 つであった。（因みに）もう 1 つは大和であった。

3. The two ships were each capable of carrying six reconnaissance aircraft.
   その 2 隻の船はお互いに 6 機の偵察機を装備する能力があった。

4. The ships had a maximum height of 56 meters, about the same as a 16-story building.
   その船は高さは最大で 56 メートル、16 階建てのビルと同じぐらいであった。

5. Naval air power was still in its early stages.
   海軍の空軍力はまだ初期段階であった。

1. The mock election helped me learn about the importance of elections.
   その模擬選挙は私が選挙の重要性を学ぶのに役立ちました。

2. A booth was set up to help students who live away from their registered residences.
   登録された住所から遠く離れたところに住む学生たちのためにブースが設営された。

3. Masui had difficulty completing the procedures necessary for casting an absentee ballot.
   Masui 氏は不在者投票に必要な手続きを完了するのに苦労した。

4. We hope to make it known that voters can cast absentee ballots.
   我々は投票者が不在者投票できるということをきちんと知らせたいと思っている。

5. The event saw a law professor specializing in electoral systems offer explanations.
   そのイベントでは選挙制度が専門の教授が色々と説明してくれる。

1．Bernard was transported from camp to camp, doing time in Auschwitz-Birkenau.
　バーナードはキャンプをあちこち連れ回され、アウシュヴィッツ強制収容所で服役した。

2．No fewer than 10 class actions have been filed against European companies.
　ヨーロッパの企業に対して集団訴訟が10件も起こされている。

3．Competing attorneys have taken to squabbling publicly.
　双方の弁護士が公開の場で口げんかを始めるというようなことが起こっている。

4．Lawyers and Jewish organizations are still hammering out the details.
　弁護士とユダヤの組織はいまだに細かな点に知恵を絞っている。

5．Yet time is not on their side.
　まだ、時は彼らの味方ではない（熟していない）。

1．Archaeology may have cast doubt on the historicity of the Old Testament characters.
　考古学的には旧約聖書の登場人物の史実性には疑いが持たれてきたかもしれない。

2．Science has neither proved nor disproved the existence of the itinerant preacher.
　科学の世界では、その巡回説教師の存在について肯定も否定もされていない。

3．The Holy Land of Jesus' time was rife with apocalyptic fervor.
　イエスの時代の聖地は黙示録の熱情（世も末だという感情）に満ち溢れていた。

4．Two members of the kibbutz came across the remains of an 8-m-long wooden dory.
　そのキブツの2人は8メートルの木製のドーリー船の残骸に出くわした。

5．Time and again, archaeological finds have validated scriptural references.
　たびたび、考古学的な発見は聖書が言及していることを検証してきた。

1．In late June, the government issued a power crunch advisory for the first time.
　6月末に、政府は初めて電力需給ひっ迫注意報を発令した。

2．The parties have been generally in agreement on expanding renewable energy sources.
　各政党は再生可能エネルギー源を拡大することについてはおおむね賛同してきた。

3．Renewable energy is not the key to maintaining a stable power supply.
　再生可能エネルギーは安定した電力需給を継続するための鍵とはならない。

4．Komeito has also put forth a policy of striving to restart nuclear reactors.
　公明党もまた、原子炉を再開する努力をするという政策を打ち出している。

5．The Japanese Communist Party has called for nuclear power to be abolished immediately.
　日本共産党は、原子力は即座に廃止するべきだとの要求を貫いている。

1. They will be loaded onto a lorry then transported to Madrid airport.
   それらはトラックに積み込まれ、マドリード空港まで輸送される。

2. On the perches are a stunning array of hybrids.
   その止まり木には、驚くべき数の雑種の鳥が並んでいる。

3. The peregrine is known as the world's fastest animal with diving speeds of up to 300kph.
   ハヤブサは世界最速の動物として知られており、急降下速度は時速 300 キロにもなる。

4. There is a sharp reprimand for the falconer who is handling them.
   それらを扱う鷹匠に対しては痛烈な批判が巻き起こっている。

5. Spain has an age-old tradition of falconry dating back to the Middle Ages.
   スペインの古来の鷹狩りの伝統は中世に遡る。

1. Former colleagues will no longer put up with unsociable evening and weekend work.
   かつての同僚たちはもはや非社交的な夕方や週末の仕事には耐えられないだろう。

2. The government has invested a lot in upskilling.
   政府は技能向上にふんだんに投資してきた。

3. There is an underlying mismatch between supply and demand.
   需要と供給の間に根本的な不整合がみられる。

4. The latter measure is designed to discourage firms from creating short-term contracts.
   後者の方策は会社に短期採用の契約を促さない目的で考え出されたものである。

5. Diners may need to get used to longer waits.
   食事客はもっと長い時間待つことに慣れる必要があるかもしれない。

1. There is no consensus on the importance of long-distance airborne transmission indoors.
   屋内での長距離の空気伝染の重要性についてはまとまった意見は出ていない。

2. They found that people can infect each other when they are more than 2 meters apart.
   2 メートル以上離れていても、お互いに感染する可能性があることが分かった。

3. Nowhere near enough is being done to ventilate public and private spaces across the world.
   世の中の公共および私的な空間の換気の対策は全く十分とは言えない状況である。

4. Having such a meter is voluntary until the end of 2024, when it becomes mandatory.
   そのようなメーターを設置するのはそれが義務化される 2024 年までは任意とされる。

5. Better ventilation can reduce the impact of pollen and other allergies.
   よりよい換気は花粉やその他のアレルギーの影響を緩和させる可能性がある。

1. Hydrogen crams more energy into less space than batteries do.
   水素は電池に比べ、小さなスペースに大きなエネルギーを詰め込める。

2. Their invention bears a passing resemblance to toothpaste.
   彼らが発明したものは、歯磨き粉に何となく似ている。

3. A third advantage is that the paste does not gradually lose its stored energy.
   3つ目の利点はそのペースト状のものは蓄積したエネルギーを逓減させないことである。

4. There are plenty of subtleties to work through.
   うまく処理しないといけない微妙な問題がたくさんある。

5. The paste is unlikely to up-end the clean-car industry.
   そのペーストはクリーンカー産業を転覆させるようなことはないであろう。

1. Mr. Bennet was capable of breathing on his own.
   ベネット氏は自力で呼吸ができた。

2. Mr. Bennet was diagnosed with terminal heart disease.
   ベネット氏は末期の心臓病と診断された。

3. Having spent months in a hospital bed, he gave his consent to the surgery.
   病院のベッドで何か月も過ごしていた彼は、その外科手術に同意した。

4. While this molecule does not exist in humans, antibodies to suppress it do.
   この分子は人体に存在しないが、それを抑制する抗体は存在する。

5. The pig in question was reared in a sterile environment to minimize the chance of that.
   当の豚（問題となっている豚）はその可能性を最小限にするため、無菌状態で育てられた。

編著者

石井　隆之（いしい　たかゆき）
近畿大学

喜多　尊史（きた　たかし）
関西大学非常勤講師

ニュース英語で世界を読み解く

2023 年 2 月 20 日　第 1 版発行

編著者──石井隆之、喜多尊史
校閲者──Ted Ostis
発行者──前田俊秀
発行所──株式会社　三修社
　　　　　〒 150-0001　東京都渋谷区神宮前 2-2-22
　　　　　TEL 03-3405-4511 / FAX 03-3405-4522
　　　　　振替 00190-9-72758
　　　　　https://www.sanshusha.co.jp/
　　　　　編集担当　伊吹和真
印刷所──萩原印刷株式会社

© 2023 printed in Japan　ISBN978-4-384-33526-2 C1082
表紙デザイン──SAIWAI Design
表紙イラスト──GreenTana（iStockphoto.com）
準拠 CD 録音──一般財団法人　英語教育協議会（ELEC）
準拠 CD 制作──高速録音株式会社
準拠 CD 吹込──Howard Colefield, Jennifer Okano

教科書準拠 CD 発売
本書の準拠 CD をご希望の方は弊社までお問い合わせください。